Starting Small:

The Raw Truth Behind Entrepreneurship and the American Dream

Copyright © 2025 by Starting Small Media

All rights reserved. No part of this publication may be reproduced, distributed, or transmitted in any form or by any means, including photocopying, recording, or other electronic or mechanical methods, without the prior written permission of the publisher, except in the case of brief quotations embodied in critical reviews and certain other noncommercial uses permitted by copyright law.

To learn more about Starting Small Media, please visit startingsmallmedia.org

Table of Contents

Dedication 1

Preface 2

Chapter 1: The Seed – Early Upbringing & Influences 7

Chapter 2: The Spark – The Problem That Led to the Idea 15

Chapter 3: Taking the Leap – Turning an Idea Into a Product 26

Chapter 4: The Hustle – Sourcing, Manufacturing & First Sales ... 36

Chapter 5: Money Matters – Funding, Bootstrapping & Early Investments 46

Chapter 6: Scaling the Chaos – Growth, Hiring & Leadership Challenges 56

Chapter 7: The Dark Side – Burnout, Failures & The Price of Success 65

Chapter 8: The Pivot – Adapting When Things Go Wrong 75

Chapter 9: The Power of Brand – How Great Companies Build Loyalty 82

Chapter 10: Marketing That Works – Strategies for Growth 91

Chapter 11: Distribution & Partnerships – Getting in Front of the Right Customers 99

Chapter 12: Customer Experience – Why It Matters More Than Anything Else 107

Chapter 13: Digital vs. Physical – Navigating E-Commerce & Retail 114

Chapter 14: The Role of Community – How Founders Leverage Their Audience 124

Chapter 15: Why are Founders Storytelling? – Selling More Than a Product 132

Chapter 16: Learning from Failure 140

Chapter 17: Exit Strategies – Selling, Acquiring, or Scaling Forever 148

Chapter 18: Finding Balance – Entrepreneurship Without Losing Yourself 156

Chapter 19: Long-Term Thinking – Playing the Infinite Game 165

Chapter 20: Lessons from 250+ Founders – Key Takeaways for Future Entrepreneurs 174

Acknowledgments 181

About The Author 182

Dedication

To Chuck Surack.

A visionary, a leader, and a mentor who accepted to be guest #1. Believed in my vision, supported our growth, and is testament to what it means to always do the right thing. Your relentless dedication to excellence, customer service, and the people around you has set the gold standard for entrepreneurship. Your story has been a guiding light—not just for me, but for countless others who believe in building something that lasts. Thank you for proving that integrity and success can go hand in hand.

LIVE from Starting Small Summit 23'

Preface

When I started **Starting Small**, I wasn't looking to build a business. I was looking for stories—the real, raw journeys behind the brands we know and love. I've always been fascinated by the people behind the products, the relentless pursuit of an idea, and the challenges no one sees. What started as a curiosity while in my sophomore year of college, turned into something much bigger: a platform that has allowed me to sit down with over 250 of the world's most impactful founders and hear firsthand how they built their brands from the ground up.

Through these conversations, one thing became clear: entrepreneurship isn't what social media makes it out to be. It's not flashy exits, overnight success, or an easy path paved with funding rounds. It's grit, resilience, sacrifice, and a constant battle between self-doubt and conviction. The founders who make it aren't always the ones with the best idea or the most money—they're the ones who refuse to quit.

This book is a culmination of those lessons. It's a reflection of the raw truth behind entrepreneurship, distilled from the wisdom of those who have lived it. Whether you're an aspiring founder, an early-stage entrepreneur, or someone looking for insight into what it really takes to build something meaningful, I hope these pages give you both clarity and motivation.

Most importantly, I hope this book serves as a reminder that the greatest companies in the world all started small. And so can you.

Introduction

In early 2020, before the world shut down, I had an idea. It wasn't grand, and it wasn't complicated. It started, like many ideas do, with curiosity. I was sitting at breakfast, staring at a syrup bottle. On the back, there was a small heritage story—just a few sentences about the brand's history. And it hit me: behind every product we use, every brand we know, there's a face, a story, a journey that we rarely get to hear.

I've always been fascinated with storytelling. In everyday conversations, I've found that people—regardless of their background—have incredible stories. But unless you ask the right questions, you'll never hear them. That morning at breakfast, I realized that no one was telling the stories behind the brands we consume daily.

So, I started a podcast.

Starting Small launched in 2020 with a simple mission: to dive deep into the journeys of entrepreneurs, uncovering the raw, unfiltered truth behind success. Since then, I've interviewed over 250 of the world's top founders and business leaders—people who have built some of the most recognizable brands across industries. From food and fashion to tech and manufacturing, these are the stories of risk-takers, problem-solvers, and relentless builders who turned small ideas into global brands.

Now, after years of conversations and lessons, it's time to put it into words—not just as a record of their journeys, but as a roadmap for yours.

There's a reason why most people never take the leap. They think they're too late. They think their idea isn't good enough. They think they aren't qualified.

But here's the truth: every single successful entrepreneur I've interviewed started exactly where you are now. In their parents' basement. At their kitchen table. Selling at farmers' markets or out of their garage. There's no golden ticket or perfect moment. The only difference between those who made it and those who didn't is that they started.

The biggest misconception about entrepreneurship is that success is reserved for a select few—those with connections, funding, or a brilliant idea from the start. But the reality is far messier. Success doesn't come from a perfect plan. It comes from action.

This book is a collection of lessons, stories, and insights from founders who started small—just like you.

It's about the struggles, the breakthroughs, and the moments that defined their journeys. It's about the unfiltered reality of entrepreneurship—the parts that don't make it into the headlines.

Whether you're thinking about starting a business, already on the journey, or simply curious about what it takes, this book is for you. My goal is to show you that success isn't about where you start—it's about taking that first step, learning along the way, and refusing to quit when things get tough.

Starting small isn't just a phase. It's a mindset. And it's the foundation of every great business.

Chapter 1

The Seed – Early Upbringing & Influences

Entrepreneurs aren't born with a road map in hand. There's no clear path drawn out for them. Instead, many successful founders find their way through a mix of early exposure to challenges, a relentless sense of curiosity, and the ability to spot opportunities where others see obstacles. The stories of some of the most iconic entrepreneurs in America didn't start in boardrooms or fancy offices. They started when they were kids, hustling on their own terms, trying to make things happen without even realizing the lessons they were learning would eventually fuel their success.

You can look at any entrepreneur's origin story and trace their motivations to moments from their early years. A lot of them never thought they were "building something" when they were doing it. They were just trying to solve problems or make something better. The real power behind those early moments, though, comes in the form of lessons learned in the trenches. These lessons come not from perfect conditions but from the gritty reality of how the world works when you're trying to make a buck on your own.

If you want to understand the DNA of a successful entrepreneur, you have to look at how they spent their formative years. What environments were they raised in? What challenges did they face? What did they learn from the people around them? All of these factors combine to lay the foundation for an entrepreneurial mindset. And the key here isn't about having access to privilege or exclusive resources—it's about how people react when they encounter adversity and how willing they are to dive into the unknown.

Take Jason Karp, for example. Jason's story doesn't start with any kind of silver spoon in his mouth. Jason's journey began with an autoimmune disease diagnosis that disrupted his life. The severity of his condition forced him to rethink everything about his lifestyle, including his health, his habits, and his perspective on the world. Instead of accepting this challenge as something he could do nothing about, he became obsessive about exploring every avenue that could provide relief. It wasn't just about his own well-being—Jason quickly realized there was an entire population out there struggling with similar health issues, many of whom were also searching for answers. His relentless commitment to improving his own health eventually led him to create Hu, a brand centered around offering clean, healthy food options that could serve a broader purpose.

The seed of his entrepreneurial journey wasn't planted in a perfect world—it was planted out of a moment of deep personal challenge. That mindset—a willingness to take matters into his own hands and find a solution—was the spark that eventually led to the creation of a company that would change the way people thought about food.

What Jason learned in his early years wasn't the typical startup playbook. Instead, he learned how to create solutions in environments where those solutions didn't exist. That early experience gave him the ability to think differently and innovate not just for himself, but for an entire community. Entrepreneurs often start their journey with the raw, unglamorous stuff: discomfort, necessity, and a little bit of grit. They don't wait for permission to create—they start with what they have and build from there.

The truth is, the best entrepreneurs aren't born with a golden ticket—they're shaped by their upbringing, yes, but also by their ability to stretch beyond their comfort zones. They learn that problems are the starting points for innovation. Whether it's a lack of resources, a broken system, or just the absence of opportunities, entrepreneurs know that limitations aren't walls—they're just hurdles that need to be jumped over or figured out.

I want to emphasize a critical point here: entrepreneurs rarely get a "perfect start." Most of them don't have families with established businesses or unlimited access to financial resources. What they do have is the ability to look at the world around them, notice things that others miss, and act on them. The best entrepreneurs are people who have mastered the art of taking small opportunities and leveraging them to create something much larger.

In fact, one of the most underrated skills in entrepreneurship is the ability to start small. Early on in their journeys, entrepreneurs learn that you don't need a massive team or tons of money to get started. You don't need a perfect product or flawless business plan. You need to take action, learn quickly, and iterate as you go. The real breakthroughs come not from waiting for the "perfect" time, but from diving in headfirst, solving problems as they arise, and adjusting along the way.

I remember hearing the story of one founder who was determined to launch a brand that would cater to a specific audience's needs, but he had no budget to work with. So, instead of going the traditional route of finding investors, he started by working out of his apartment, creating prototypes on his own, and selling his products out of the back of his car. He didn't start with millions of dollars or a polished marketing strategy. He started with the resources he had, which was his own time, energy, and creativity.

That's how most entrepreneurs start—the journey begins with hustle, a willingness to work hard, and an unwavering belief that the solution to a problem exists somewhere, and they'll be the ones to find it. There's no glamorous story here. It's about someone grinding it out, staying up late, and doing the work. The path isn't paved with ease—it's made with the grit and perseverance that comes from being willing to put everything on the line for an idea you believe in.

Entrepreneurs also start early, and often, they don't even know they're starting. That's one of the most fascinating aspects of entrepreneurial journeys. The seeds are planted in childhood, in ways that many of us don't even recognize until later in life. I've spoken with several founders who, when asked about their first business venture, shared stories of selling things on eBay or starting small service businesses like dog walking or lawn care. These might seem like small ventures, but they all teach valuable lessons about the importance of sales, marketing, and customer service.

The best entrepreneurs are the ones who have figured out that you don't need a "big" idea to start. You just need to start. You need to get your hands dirty, learn the process, and keep improving along the way. Each of those early experiences adds to the toolkit that they'll use later when they scale up.

There's a reason why so many successful entrepreneurs didn't follow the traditional path. For them, the idea of following a conventional career trajectory didn't resonate. They needed something else—something that required them to break free from what they were told they "should" be doing and instead figure out what they *wanted* to do. They needed to step into the unknown, to be uncomfortable, and to take risks. That's where the real magic happens.

A common thread in all these stories is how early life challenges shape entrepreneurs. From navigating difficult financial circumstances to simply figuring out how to make things work with limited resources, many entrepreneurs grew up learning how to make the most out of what they had. These experiences—whether they involved figuring out how to make extra money on the side, or having to help support their family—create a level of resourcefulness that's difficult to replicate in any classroom.

But it's not just about hardship or limited means. Even entrepreneurs who grew up with financial stability and resources still learn lessons from their upbringing that shape their business acumen. It's the values they're taught—the importance of hard work, the ability to take initiative, the value of empathy, and understanding that no job is too small—that often sets the stage for the mindset they bring to their businesses. These aren't qualities that you can easily teach in a business school course. They come from life experiences, from being told "no" or watching a parent hustle to make ends meet.

One thing I've learned from talking to hundreds of founders is that the best entrepreneurs are the ones who view challenges as opportunities for growth. They look at problems as chances to innovate, to think creatively, and to make things better. Entrepreneurship, at its core, is a mindset—a way of looking at the world and recognizing opportunities where others see roadblocks. The entrepreneurs I've interviewed didn't sit back and wait for the world to serve them—they went out and built the world they wanted to see.

So, when you're thinking about entrepreneurship, don't just think about the big ideas. Think about the small moments, the everyday challenges, and the way those moments prepare you for the bigger journey ahead. If you want to build something, you've got to start somewhere. And often, that somewhere is messy, chaotic, and imperfect. But that's where the magic begins.

grow into something much bigger.

"Listen to learn, but keep thinking differently."

-Cameron Smith, Co-Founder of Kodiak Cakes

Chapter 2

The Spark – The Problem That Led to the Idea

Every great business starts with a problem. Not just any problem, but one that either disrupts a person's daily life or one that exposes a glaring inefficiency in the world. Sometimes it's an inconvenience that, when seen through the eyes of an entrepreneur, transforms into an opportunity. Sometimes it's a frustration that triggers a realization. And sometimes, it's something so simple that it's easy to overlook—yet it holds the key to creating something bigger than you ever imagined. That's when the spark happens—the precise moment when an entrepreneur sees an issue, recognizes it as a problem that needs solving, and realizes that they might just have the solution.

It's easy to look at successful companies today and think that the idea came from some massive strategy meeting or some carefully constructed business plan. But most of the time, the journey to building a thriving business didn't start with money or ambition—it started with a simple realization that something wasn't right. That something, if fixed, could make life better for a lot of people. This recognition is where it all begins.

Entrepreneurs don't wake up with grand ambitions to build a billion-dollar company. What they wake up with is frustration, the realization that there is a solution waiting to be discovered. And often, that solution is based on something deeply personal, something they themselves have struggled with. It's not about trying to revolutionize the world overnight; it's about addressing something in their own lives that needs fixing. From there, they begin to think—what if this isn't just a problem for me? What if other people have the same issue?

Look at Airbnb, for example. The founders didn't start with an elaborate business plan or venture capital backing. They started with a simple problem: they couldn't afford rent. So, they thought, why not rent out air mattresses in their living room to make ends meet? At the time, the solution seemed small—more of a short-term fix than a long-term business strategy. But that small problem-solving approach led them to discover something much larger. As it turned out, other people were willing to pay to stay in someone's home. And that was the spark. They stumbled upon a simple idea that not only solved their problem, but it solved a much bigger problem for many others—finding affordable, alternative places to stay. They didn't start with the grand vision of disrupting the hotel industry—they started with a personal problem. From that, everything else evolved.

This is a consistent theme in the stories of many successful entrepreneurs. They aren't necessarily trying to create something world-changing from day one. Instead, they focus on fixing a problem they've experienced personally. And in doing so, they end up solving that problem for countless others. This problem-solving mindset, the willingness to take action and offer a solution to the issue at hand, is what drives most entrepreneurial ventures.

Take Sara Blakely, the founder of Spanx. Sara's journey didn't begin with an in-depth market study or years of industry experience. It began with a very personal problem: finding the right undergarment. She was frustrated by the lack of comfortable, functional shapewear that could meet her needs. She looked at the market and saw a gap—nothing offered the level of comfort and function she was looking for. So, she took matters into her own hands. She didn't wait for some grand breakthrough or investor funding. She started with a simple solution to her problem. The result? Spanx, one of the most successful and recognized brands in the world today. She didn't just solve her own problem—she solved it for millions of women, changing the way people think about undergarments forever.

This type of approach isn't just about being opportunistic. It's about noticing what the market is missing and taking steps to fill that gap. Entrepreneurs who start businesses based on solving their own problems often find that their solutions resonate with a larger audience. It's about recognizing that your frustration or inconvenience is likely shared by others. The ability to spot this gap and then take action on it is what separates entrepreneurs from non-entrepreneurs. When a founder sees a problem, they don't just shake their head and move on—they begin to think about how they can fix it. And, in doing so, they begin the process of building something bigger.

The story of Stacy Madison, the founder of Stacy's Pita Chips, is another example of how this realization can lead to something much larger than originally expected. Stacy wasn't a seasoned snack industry veteran when she started her business. She and her partner were running a small food cart in Boston, selling sandwiches. To keep customers occupied while they waited in line, they started baking extra pita bread into chips and handing them out for free. The feedback was immediate: people loved the chips. In fact, they loved them so much that they began asking if they could buy them. Stacy, who hadn't originally set out to start a snack company, saw a clear opportunity. The chips weren't just a free snack for waiting customers—they were the core of her business. And that's when it clicked. Stacy didn't plan to be in the snack business. She was just reacting to what customers were telling her. Her business idea was born not from a traditional business strategy, but from a direct response to customer demand. She listened, adapted, and took action.

This is one of the most powerful lessons an entrepreneur can learn: always listen to your customers. Often, the business you think you're starting isn't the one that ends up being successful. The key is to be flexible enough to pivot when you spot a bigger opportunity. Stacy Madison didn't get so fixated on her original idea (selling sandwiches) that she missed the clear opportunity in front of her (selling pita chips). This is where a lot of businesses fail—they get too wrapped up in their original vision and don't pivot when they see a better option. Stacy, on the other hand, was open to changing course, and that decision ultimately led her to build a multimillion-dollar brand.

Sometimes, the path to success isn't linear. It's full of twists and turns. The best entrepreneurs are the ones who are willing to adapt. Take Hap Klopp's journey with The North Face. When Hap first launched The North Face, he wasn't trying to build a global outdoor brand. He simply saw a problem in the outdoor equipment industry. Adventurers were using subpar gear that failed in the toughest conditions. He knew this wasn't just inconvenient—it was dangerous. So, he set out to create equipment that could withstand the harshest environments, whether it was the freezing cold of a mountain or the intense heat of a desert. The North Face wasn't born out of a desire to be the biggest brand in the world; it was born out of a desire to fix a critical problem—adventurers weren't properly equipped to stay safe.

This is an important takeaway for aspiring entrepreneurs: it's not just about having a good idea—it's about recognizing when that idea isn't enough and being willing to evolve it. Entrepreneurs who succeed don't get stuck on their original idea—they iterate, pivot, and improve along the way. That's the difference between a business that fizzles out and one that thrives for the long haul.

Of course, having an idea is only the beginning. Execution is everything. Once an entrepreneur identifies the problem they want to solve, they must then turn that idea into a viable product or service. Ideas without execution are just dreams. Entrepreneurs who succeed are those who take action. They don't wait for perfect conditions; they start with what they have. They make progress, no matter how small, and refine their business model as they go.

The first steps are often messy. There is no magic moment where everything falls into place. The most successful entrepreneurs understand that. They don't wait for perfection before taking action—they move forward, even when things are uncertain. The key to success is the ability to act, even when you don't have all the answers.

One of the biggest misconceptions about entrepreneurship is that successful business owners have everything figured out from day one. They don't. The real difference between successful and unsuccessful entrepreneurs is their willingness to start, even when things aren't perfect. Many founders talk about how they didn't know exactly what they were doing in the beginning. But they kept moving forward anyway. They didn't wait for everything to be ideal—they embraced the messiness of the process and learned as they went.

Too many people talk themselves out of their ideas before they even start. They convince themselves they aren't ready. They think they need more experience, more money, more resources. But the truth is, those things will come with time. What you need to start is the willingness to act. Don't wait for the perfect moment, because it will never come. Start where you are, with what you have, and build from there. That's how successful businesses are created—one imperfect step at a time.

The difference between the dreamers and the doers is simple: the doers take action. They recognize a problem, take the first step, and keep moving forward, even when it's hard. Entrepreneurs who succeed are the ones who take that initial spark of an idea and transform it into something real. They don't let fear, doubt, or imperfection stop them. They keep going, adjusting, and refining their ideas until they've built something that works.

So, the next time you come across a problem, don't dismiss it as just another inconvenience. Ask yourself, is this something I could solve? Is there an opportunity here? The spark of an idea is just the beginning. What matters most is how you act on it. Start small, take imperfect action, and adjust as you go. And remember, the only thing standing between you and success is the willingness to take that first step.

"The WHO should be before the WHAT. Who is benefiting and who is on board."

-Nirav Tolia, Founder of Nextdoor

Chapter 3

Taking the Leap – Turning an Idea Into a Product

Every successful business starts with a problem. Recognizing that problem, spotting an opportunity, or identifying a gap in the market can feel like the most important part. It's the "aha moment" where the puzzle pieces fall into place. But let me tell you, recognizing a great idea is one thing. Acting on it? That's entirely different. This is where so many aspiring entrepreneurs get stuck.

What often follows the initial spark of an idea is a flood of emotions: self-doubt, fear of failure, uncertainty about where to start, and confusion about how to proceed. For many, the leap from idea to execution feels like jumping off a cliff without a parachute. But the truth is, no successful founder had all the answers when they started. What they did have was a willingness to jump and trust that the answers would come along the way.

Taking the leap doesn't always mean quitting your day job or diving headfirst into a full-blown operation. It doesn't even mean risking everything you have in one shot. In fact, some of the most successful brands in the world started as side projects—small, cautious experiments that slowly gained momentum before the founders went all-in. You don't need to take on the whole world at once. The key is to start in any capacity possible. It doesn't matter if that means testing your product on a micro scale, gathering feedback, or refining it along the way.

The Power of Starting Small

Consider the story of Jaime Schmidt, the founder of Schmidt's Naturals. Jaime's entrepreneurial journey didn't begin with a big corporate background or massive financial backing. Instead, she was a mom searching for a better, more natural deodorant for her family. Like many founders, Jaime had no formal training in product development or business management. What she did have was a strong desire to solve a problem, and that led her to experiment with natural formulas right in her own kitchen.

Jaime didn't launch with a full product line or millions of dollars in funding. She started by creating small batches of deodorant and selling them at local farmers' markets. There were no guarantees. No one knew if the market even wanted a natural alternative to commercial deodorants. But Jaime took the risk, she tested the waters, and as she began receiving feedback, she refined her product.

Her approach wasn't flashy or immediate, but it worked. Over time, Schmidt's Naturals gained traction, and with that momentum, Jaime took the leap—building a multimillion-dollar business that was ultimately acquired by Unilever. She didn't rush the process. Her success came from starting small, validating her product in the market, and letting the business grow organically.

The lesson here? It's not about having the perfect product from day one. It's about starting and learning as you go. Your business idea doesn't need to be fully baked. Get it out there, see what people think, and iterate. Start with what you have, and work towards the rest.

Taking Calculated Steps

Another founder who embodies the principle of starting small is Daniel Winer of HexClad. Daniel's approach to launching HexClad, a revolutionary cookware brand, wasn't rushed. Instead of jumping in with a full line of products and massive manufacturing commitments, he and his team tested different materials, perfected their hybrid – stainless/nonstick technology, and made sure that when they launched, they had something truly game-changing to offer.

HexClad didn't explode onto the scene overnight. It was the result of careful planning, testing, and validating a product with potential before scaling production. Daniel didn't wait for perfection, but he also didn't rush into a hasty launch either. He understood the importance of product-market fit and how it can make or break your brand.

One of the most crucial steps in the process of taking the leap is to **validate before you scale**. This is often overlooked in the excitement of starting a business. The first step in your entrepreneurial journey should be to test and refine. Ask questions. Get feedback. Understand the real-world demand for your product or service before diving into large-scale operations. Daniel didn't flood the market with thousands of products before he knew there was a demand. Instead, he focused on quality and customer satisfaction, taking calculated steps and refining the product until it could stand up to the hype.

Overcoming Skepticism and Doubt

Along with practical concerns, every entrepreneur faces a mental barrier: the fear of failure. It's natural to be nervous, to doubt yourself, and to wonder whether you're truly cut out for the journey. In fact, the vast majority of entrepreneurs face skepticism—both from external sources like family and friends and from internal sources in the form of their own doubts and insecurities.

The most successful founders understand that doubt and discomfort are part of the journey. They recognize it and keep moving forward regardless. In fact, many entrepreneurs actively lean into discomfort. They know that growth comes when they're willing to step into the unknown.

The Secret to Overcoming Fear: Action

One of the best ways to beat self-doubt is by taking action, no matter how small. You don't need to know everything to get started. Every small action you take—whether that's creating a prototype, having a conversation with a potential customer, or getting your first sale—builds momentum. It helps you push past your doubts and gives you the confidence to continue moving forward.

A common pitfall for new entrepreneurs is waiting for perfection. They keep refining their product, overthinking their strategy, and waiting for the "perfect" moment to launch. But I'm here to tell you: waiting for perfection will kill your business before it even starts. Perfection doesn't exist when you're starting out. There's no such thing as the perfect product, the perfect marketing strategy, or the perfect business plan. The most successful entrepreneurs are the ones who take **imperfect action**. They jump into the unknown, and they adjust as they go.

Betting on Yourself

Taking the leap also requires sacrifice. Many founders talk about sleepless nights, financial struggles, and missed social events as they focus on getting their businesses off the ground. It's not all glamour and excitement in the early stages—there's a lot of grit involved. You'll likely face moments where you wonder whether it's all worth it. You'll question if you made the right decision.

But the founders who succeed are the ones who **bet on themselves**. They take the leap even when there's no guarantee of success. The ones who succeed are willing to make sacrifices, put in the work, and keep pushing forward when everything seems uncertain.

The road isn't easy, and it's not meant to be. No one ever said building a business was going to be smooth sailing. But the ones who succeed don't back down when things get tough. They double down on their commitment and find a way to move forward. Sometimes, that's a sacrifice of time; other times, it's a financial risk. But every sacrifice is an investment in your future.

From Idea to Reality: The Logistics of Execution

Another major obstacle for many aspiring entrepreneurs is the logistical side of bringing an idea to life. How do you manufacture? How do you handle packaging, shipping, and inventory? What about the legalities of registering a business, handling trademarks, and managing taxes? The unknowns here are overwhelming for many, and often this is where people get paralyzed and give up.

But here's the truth: you'll figure it out as you go. It's one of the biggest misconceptions of entrepreneurship to think you need to have every detail planned out before you take the first step. Sure, you need a basic structure, but you don't need to have every step mapped out for the next 10 years. The logistics of creating and delivering a product often come with a huge learning curve, and yes, you'll make mistakes. But you'll learn, adjust, and keep moving forward.

Joe Foster of Reebok, saw an opportunity in the running shoe industry and didn't have the luxury of global manufacturing networks or massive distribution channels. Instead, he started by learning every step of the process firsthand. Joe didn't rush into scaling his operations. He focused on learning and refining his approach before expanding. Reebok didn't become a global powerhouse overnight—it took years of persistence, tweaking, and trial and error.

Similarly, Stacy Madison, didn't envision herself building a snack empire. She simply started baking extra pita bread into chips for customers waiting in line at her food cart. The demand for her chips grew organically, and she responded. What started as a small, organic idea turned into a multi-million dollar business because Stacy acted on the opportunity she saw in front of her.

Evolving Over Time

Another key point to consider when taking the leap is understanding that you don't need to have everything figured out from the start. Too many would-be entrepreneurs delay their launch because they think they need a fully realized business plan or product. But successful businesses don't emerge as perfectly formed entities. They evolve over time.

Take Jason Karp, co-founder of Hu Chocolate. When he and his team set out to create a healthier chocolate brand, they didn't start by producing thousands of bars and flooding the market. Instead, they worked through multiple iterations, testing small batches, tweaking recipes, and building an audience before committing to a large-scale launch. By the time Hu gained national recognition, the company had already put in the work to ensure that the product aligned with consumer demands. Their slow, methodical approach allowed them to scale successfully without getting ahead of themselves.

The Inevitable Failures

Finally, one of the most important aspects of taking the leap is understanding that failure is a part of the process. Every entrepreneur faces setbacks. Whether it's a product launch that doesn't go as planned, a marketing campaign that misses the mark, or a financial hurdle that seems insurmountable, failure is inevitable.

But the founders who succeed are the ones who push forward in spite of these failures. They treat each setback as a learning opportunity, and instead of letting it stop them, they use it to refine their approach.

As I've heard time and time again from the entrepreneurs I've interviewed, the key to success is **just starting**. Stop overanalyzing. Stop waiting for permission. Stop convincing yourself you're not ready. You will never feel 100% ready to start your business. And that's okay. The most successful entrepreneurs take imperfect action, make adjustments as they go, and keep moving forward.

At the end of the day, **taking the leap** isn't about having the perfect plan. It's about starting. No business launches flawlessly. No founder has all the answers from day one. The only way to figure it out is to step into the unknown, start small, and adjust as you go. The only thing holding you back is yourself. So go ahead — take the leap.

"Expect the difficulties, but look out for the luck. Don't let it pass you by."

-Joe Foster, Founder of Reebok

Chapter 4

The Hustle – Sourcing, Manufacturing & First Sales

Turning an idea into a tangible product is the moment when your entrepreneurial journey transitions from the realm of dreams and concepts to the reality of the marketplace. It's the point where the excitement of having a great idea meets the grind of logistics, production, and the overwhelming task of getting that product into customers' hands. While the vision of a new business is often exhilarating, the process of turning that vision into something real can be grueling, frustrating, and full of unexpected challenges. For many entrepreneurs, this stage is filled with self-doubt, and it's easy to question whether it will ever happen. It's not just about having the right idea; it's about learning how to manufacture it, sell it, and refine it—sometimes in ways you never expected.

Sourcing materials and manufacturing the product is one of the first major hurdles you'll face, and it's often where many businesses start to either find their feet or stumble. When you're just starting out, you don't have a wealth of experience to draw from, so everything feels like a new challenge. Where do you source your materials? Do you go local or offshore? Should you bootstrap production, or is it better to seek outside investment? And, perhaps the most critical question: how do you find a manufacturer who can deliver on time and at the right cost? These are not easy questions to answer, but the businesses that succeed find ways to navigate through them, one step at a time.

Take Stacy Madison. Her journey didn't start with a massive manufacturing plant or a polished supply chain. It started with a sandwich cart business, and baking pita chips was just something extra she did for customers while they waited. At first, it was a side project, but when demand for her chips grew, she had to figure out how to produce them on a larger scale. The challenge wasn't just about baking more chips; it was about finding a manufacturer who could handle the growing demand, learning food production laws, and keeping the quality consistent. She had no formal training in food production—she was a small business owner trying to figure out the logistics as she went. It was messy and uncertain, but ultimately, it worked because she kept pushing forward, figuring things out one step at a time.

Think about Joe Foster of Reebok. When Joe saw the opportunity to revolutionize the running shoe market, he didn't have the luxury of huge resources at his disposal. He started by working with a small family-owned factory. However, as Reebok grew, he encountered the same challenges that many new founders face: factories that couldn't meet deadlines, materials that failed testing, and shipping delays that threatened to halt production altogether. Reebok wasn't built overnight, and the company's early days were filled with trial and error. Joe had to learn how to manage his suppliers and constantly tweak his manufacturing process. He didn't have everything figured out from day one—he learned as he went, building relationships with reliable suppliers, adjusting his approach when things went wrong, and finding ways to keep the business moving forward.

Most entrepreneurs will face the same kinds of frustrations when it comes to manufacturing and production. Initial prototypes are often far from perfect. Materials sometimes fail to meet expectations, and you might even get stuck with huge minimum order quantities that eat up your limited cash flow. When the products finally do arrive, they might be damaged, defective, or just not what you envisioned. These are the growing pains that most founders encounter. The difference between those who make it and those who don't is how they handle these challenges. Founders who succeed aren't the ones who avoid problems — they're the ones who face them head-on, learn from their mistakes, and continue to refine their processes.

Once you've found your suppliers, developed your product, and navigated the minefield of manufacturing, the next challenge is sales. For bootstrapped founders, large marketing budgets and expensive ad campaigns are often out of the question. So, the question becomes: how do you get your first sales, and more importantly, how do you validate the market demand for your product without spending all your money upfront?

Jaime Schmidt's story shows you how to navigate this stage. She didn't land in big-box stores right away. Instead, she started by selling her natural deodorant at local farmers' markets. She had no outside funding and no big marketing budget, but she knew that real customers — people who actually paid for her product — would give her valuable feedback. She used these interactions to refine her formula, improving it based on what customers liked and didn't like. By selling directly to customers, she could reinvest every dollar back into growing the business. This allowed her to scale at a sustainable pace, building her brand gradually as the product proved itself in the marketplace. Jaime didn't wait for perfection; she started small and let the market guide her decisions.

Daniel Daniel Winer of HexClad took a different approach but still embraced the power of direct-to-consumer sales. Rather than relying on traditional retail routes, Daniel focused on leveraging digital marketing and social media to build his brand and connect directly with consumers. HexClad intentionally shied away from a traditional brick and mortar strategy. Instead, Daniel Daniel and his team focused on building a digital-first brand, establishing an online presence, robust PR, and growing through word-of-mouth marketing and online sales. By avoiding traditional retail routes, Daniel was able to maintain strong margins and build direct relationships with customers, ultimately scaling the business in a way that fit his vision.

The first sale is a pivotal moment for any entrepreneur. It's when the idea shifts from abstract to tangible—it's when you realize that someone, somewhere, believes in what you've created. But getting from one sale to hundreds, thousands, or millions takes hustle. The first sale is just the beginning; the real challenge is how to repeat that success, over and over again. In the early days, this requires hands-on effort. Many founders pack their own orders, handle customer service calls, and respond to every email themselves. It's exhausting, but it's also a rite of passage. Selling is not just about pushing a product—it's about storytelling. People don't just buy a product; they buy into your brand, your mission, and your vision as a founder. Founders who succeed early on are those who can communicate why their product matters and how it can solve a real problem for their customers.

Another major challenge at this stage is pricing. Many new entrepreneurs make the mistake of pricing their products too low, assuming that lower prices will automatically attract more customers. This can backfire. Pricing too low can signal to potential customers that your product is cheap or low quality. Moreover, without adequate profit margins, scaling the business becomes incredibly difficult. The key to pricing is understanding your costs—production, shipping, marketing, customer acquisition—and then ensuring that your prices reflect the value you offer. You can't build a sustainable business on razor-thin margins, so it's critical to factor in all your costs and price your products accordingly. Successful founders know that pricing is a balancing act. It's not just about being competitive; it's about making sure your business is financially viable in the long run.

One of the most important lessons from this stage is that no one has it all figured out in the beginning. The founders who appear to have overnight success often have years of refinement, trial and error, and overcoming setbacks behind them. It's easy to look at a company that's succeeded and think they had it all figured out from day one, but the truth is that most successful entrepreneurs spend a lot of time figuring things out along the way. They make mistakes, learn from them, and adjust their approach as they go. What separates those who succeed from those who don't isn't a lack of challenges—it's the willingness to keep going despite those challenges.

Launching a product is rarely smooth. Manufacturing is rarely seamless. Sales are almost always unpredictable. But this stage is also when a business is truly born. It's when an idea becomes something that people can touch, buy, and use. If you can weather the frustrations of production, the setbacks of manufacturing, and the grind of getting your first sales, you're on the path to building something real. The key is persistence. It's about embracing the messiness, learning from the mistakes, and finding a way to make things work. Because at the end of the day, no business truly exists until someone buys your product. The road from idea to product is full of challenges, but the ones who make it are those who embrace those challenges, adapt, and keep pushing forward.

"Embrace economic pressure to make you keep going."

-Shawn Nelson, Founder of Lovesac

Chapter 5

Money Matters – Funding, Bootstrapping & Early Investments

One of the most pressing questions new entrepreneurs face is how to fund their business. Should they bootstrap and rely on personal savings? Should they seek out investors? Take out loans? The financial aspect of launching a company can feel overwhelming, and the decisions made during this phase often determine how a business scales—or whether it survives at all.

Many aspiring founders believe they need massive investment to start their businesses, and the thought of securing outside capital often dominates their focus. Yet, some of the most successful companies today started with very little external funding. Jaime Schmidt, for example, started Schmidt's Naturals with only a few hundred dollars. She relied on reinvesting profits from early sales to fuel growth and stayed lean during her company's formative years. This strategy of scrappiness, combined with the discipline to avoid unnecessary expenses, helped Schmidt build a multimillion-dollar company without ever taking on outside investment. Her story is a testament to the potential of bootstrapping—a route that offers autonomy and control.

However, not all businesses can start without outside capital. Some ideas require significant investment to get off the ground, especially when scaling is part of the plan. Joe Foster, for instance, recognized that in order to make Reebok a global brand, he needed funding for production and distribution. His experience highlights a critical lesson in knowing when to seek funding and how to pitch the business effectively to investors. Whether it's venture capital, angel investors, or traditional loans, seeking financial support comes with its own set of challenges—chief among them the pressure to scale quickly.

When bootstrapping, the major advantage is maintaining full control over the business. Founders can grow at their own pace, making decisions based on their vision without the pressure of answering to outside investors. However, bootstrapping also carries its limitations. Without external funds, scaling can be slower, and the founder often bears the financial burden personally. Entrepreneurs who choose this path must be resourceful, constantly finding creative ways to market their products, negotiate with suppliers, and make strategic decisions that support long-term growth with limited funds.

One of the core principles of bootstrapping is financial discipline. Cash flow is the lifeblood of any business, and every dollar counts. Founders who succeed in the bootstrapping route are often meticulous about how they allocate their resources. For example, Stacy Madison of Stacy's Pita Chips didn't rush into large-scale production. Instead, she strategically reinvested the profits from early sales, allowing her business to grow gradually while avoiding debt or outside investment. This method kept her in control and allowed her to retain ownership of the company when she eventually sold it. Her approach is an example of how patience and careful financial planning can lead to long-term success.

For many entrepreneurs, securing external funding feels like a necessary step. Raising capital can help scale a business more rapidly, increase production capabilities, or facilitate marketing efforts. But raising money comes with its own set of challenges. Most investors expect a return on their investment, which means the entrepreneur faces pressure to prioritize short-term growth at the cost of long-term sustainability. This can lead to difficult decisions, as many business founders are torn between growing rapidly and maintaining control over their company's direction.

It's easy to believe that raising large amounts of money will lead to success. But many entrepreneurs who succeed are the ones who manage their funding wisely, even after they've secured it. Some successful founders emphasize the importance of staying scrappy, even after receiving investment. They remind us that just because there's money in the bank doesn't mean it should be spent recklessly. Instead, funds should be allocated to areas that generate the most impact. When funds are raised, the key is to use them strategically. This means focusing on the critical elements that will help scale the business—whether it's improving the product, hiring the right team members, or marketing the brand effectively.

Raising too much capital too soon can be a pitfall for entrepreneurs. While it might seem like a blessing to have a large budget at the outset, it often leads to wasteful spending. Overhiring, investing in unnecessary infrastructure, or spending too much on marketing too early can dilute the potential for sustainable growth. Some of the most successful founders in the world have raised small amounts at the right time, using those funds to test their products, refine their processes, and scale when they were ready, rather than being driven by an arbitrary goal of securing large investments.

When it comes to seeking outside investment, the options can be overwhelming. Many new entrepreneurs immediately think of venture capital as the best route to scaling their business. But venture capital (VC) is not always the best fit for every company. VC funding is designed for companies with the potential for rapid, massive growth. Investors expect a high return, and they're often looking for companies that can quickly expand into global markets. Not every business fits that mold, and in those cases, VC funding might not be appropriate.

Angel investors, on the other hand, may be more open to providing funding in the early stages of a company. Angel investors often provide capital in exchange for equity, but they tend to be more flexible and patient than venture capitalists. Many angel investors are willing to take a chance on an idea or a founder they believe in, even if the business doesn't yet have a proven track record. These investors can be valuable partners who bring not just capital but also experience and mentorship.

Crowdfunding has become an increasingly popular way for startups to raise money, especially for product-based businesses. Platforms like Kickstarter and Indiegogo allow entrepreneurs to present their ideas to the public, offering early access to products in exchange for financial backing. Crowdfunding provides more than just funding; it offers market validation before full-scale production begins. A successful crowdfunding campaign proves that there's real demand for the product, which can be critical for a startup's credibility.

While crowdfunding can be a great way to get off the ground, it's not a guaranteed route to success. Entrepreneurs need to invest time and effort into creating compelling campaigns that resonate with potential backers. It's essential to clearly articulate the value proposition, provide updates throughout the campaign, and deliver on promises to backers once the funds are raised.

Government grants and small business loans are another avenue that entrepreneurs often overlook. Many governments offer low-interest loans, grants, or tax incentives to support startups and small businesses. Unlike venture capital, government-backed loans don't require giving up equity, which makes them a safer option for entrepreneurs who want to maintain control over their business. The downside is that the application process for grants and loans can be competitive and time-consuming.

Once the money is secured, the next challenge is managing it effectively. Financial mismanagement is one of the leading causes of business failure. Entrepreneurs who fail to track their cash flow, monitor expenses, and plan for the future often find themselves in financial trouble. But the best founders know that every decision—whether it's marketing spend, employee salaries, or operational costs—impacts the bottom line. They stay financially literate, understand how to balance profit margins with costs, and maximize the efficiency of every dollar spent.

For many entrepreneurs, the key to success lies in stretching every dollar. They negotiate better terms with suppliers, limit overhead costs, and reinvest profits carefully. Instead of splurging on lavish office spaces or unnecessary hires, they prioritize spending that drives growth. Every dollar is allocated toward making the business stronger—whether through product development, marketing, or hiring a key employee who can drive the company forward.

Stacy Madison, founder of Stacy's Pita Chips, is a great example of a founder who practiced financial discipline. When she started her company, she focused on gradual scaling, reinvesting profits at every stage of growth. This careful approach allowed her to build a solid foundation and scale sustainably, eventually leading to a profitable exit when the company was sold. Her story illustrates the value of patience and restraint—two essential qualities for any founder navigating the financial landscape of entrepreneurship.

As an entrepreneur, it's essential to treat any investment money like your own personal savings. Whether bootstrapping or taking on outside investment, the key is to use resources thoughtfully. The best founders allocate funding to areas that will have the greatest impact, rather than relying on outside capital as a crutch.

Another key takeaway is that fundraising isn't a quick fix. It's time-consuming and often involves months of meetings, pitches, and negotiations. Many founders hear "no" far more often than they hear "yes," and rejections can be discouraging. But these moments are opportunities to refine the business model, strengthen the pitch, and build resilience. Investors aren't just looking for a good idea—they're looking for a founder who can demonstrate passion, drive, and the ability to execute.

Whether an entrepreneur chooses to bootstrap or seek investment, the underlying principle remains the same: financial discipline is crucial to success. Smart founders don't just think about raising money—they think about how to use that money to grow strategically and sustainably. They understand that growth is a marathon, not a sprint. Successful entrepreneurs treat every dollar like an investment in the future, and they know that no matter which route they choose to fund their business, the goal is always the same: to build a profitable, sustainable business that lasts for the long haul.

"Have a business plan, but listen to what's coming back from the marketplace."

-Hap Klopp, Founder of The North Face

Chapter 6

Scaling the Chaos – Growth, Hiring & Leadership Challenges

Scaling a business is one of the most exhilarating yet daunting phases of entrepreneurship. It's when the dream of growing a small venture into something larger begins to unfold, but it's also the moment when everything starts to get more complicated. While the early days of starting a business often feel like a continuous hustle—launching a product, securing a few initial sales, and having an intimate connection with your customers—scaling forces you to face new and far more complex challenges. It's a stage where growth can quickly tip from exciting to overwhelming, and the stakes get higher with every decision.

What makes scaling so challenging is that it requires an entirely different set of skills. What worked when you were operating as a lean, small startup—being the jack-of-all-trades, controlling everything from product development to marketing—no longer applies. The processes that got you to where you are may not be scalable. That exciting period of being deeply involved in every aspect of the business fades into the background, as new pressures arise. The excitement is often accompanied by stress, confusion, and a feeling of drowning under the weight of everything that needs to get done.

One of the largest challenges during the scaling phase, often making or breaking businesses, is the hiring process. In the beginning, founders typically start with a small, tight-knit team or even handle everything themselves. However, as demand grows, the realization dawns that you can't do it all anymore. You're simply stretched too thin to keep up with your ambitions. As a result, you must begin building a team. But the question is, who do you hire? Finding the right people is not just about filling positions—it's about finding the right people who are not only competent but who fit into the culture you've created and help drive the company toward its vision. A bad hire at this stage can have serious consequences, draining resources, delaying progress, and creating internal friction. It can even threaten your company's core values.

The mistake many entrepreneurs make when hiring during the scaling process is rushing the decision. The pressure to fill positions quickly often leads to hiring someone based on their resume or experience rather than assessing whether they truly understand the vision, are capable of adapting to the company's needs, and will be able to handle the unpredictable nature of a growing business. Joe Foster, the founder of Reebok, faced this exact issue when scaling his company. When Reebok started to gain momentum, he found himself in need of people who understood global expansion—a realm he had little experience in. But in order to scale properly, he knew he had to bring in expertise in this area, even though it took some trial and error along the way. By hiring people who understood global distribution, manufacturing, and international sales, Reebok could secure deals that helped it expand globally and eventually become one of the most recognized athletic brands in the world.

At the same time, there's another side to scaling a business—the lean and strategic approach. Jaime Schmidt, the founder of Schmidt's Naturals, took a slightly different route. She prioritized cultural fit and adaptability over sheer experience when hiring her team. Schmidt's was able to grow steadily while maintaining a close-knit, strong company culture. For Jaime, hiring people who were passionate about natural products and understood the brand's ethos was more important than simply filling roles with people who had the most experience. Her team's dedication to the company's mission was key to Schmidt's success, and by focusing on cultural fit, she ensured that the company remained true to its core even as it scaled to meet increasing demand.

While hiring the right people is paramount to scaling, another significant hurdle is maintaining the quality and consistency of your product. When you're operating at a small scale, you have full control over every detail. But when your business starts growing rapidly, the very systems and processes that worked when you were a one- or two-person operation can quickly break down. The struggle to maintain quality while meeting growing demand can turn into a nightmare if you don't take proactive steps to address it. Process development, strict quality control measures, and standardization are crucial to scaling successfully. Otherwise, a slip-up in quality control or product consistency can undermine everything you've worked for.

Take Daniel Winer, the founder of HexClad, for example. As his cookware company gained traction and orders multiplied, maintaining quality became a critical issue. HexClad's success hinged on the brand's commitment to providing cookware that met the highest standards. But as they scaled, ensuring every pan met those same rigorous standards became increasingly difficult. Daniel could have been tempted to cut corners to meet growing demand, but he understood that compromising on quality would lead to negative reviews, returns, and a damaged reputation. Instead, he chose to invest in meticulous quality assurance practices, ensuring that each product met the brand's stringent standards. This decision ultimately helped HexClad continue to thrive even as demand grew exponentially.

Quality is not just about the product itself—it's also about the experience surrounding the product. This is another reason why scaling is so challenging. As your business grows, so do customer expectations. In the early stages, you may be able to personally interact with every customer or handle customer service yourself. But as your customer base grows, that level of personal attention becomes impossible. The key challenge is maintaining the level of service and quality your customers have come to expect while expanding operations. And this brings us to another key aspect of scaling: leadership.

Many entrepreneurs are excellent at the building phase. They're visionaries and doers, focused on making their idea come to life. But as the business scales, the founder's role inevitably shifts. You're no longer the person doing everything—now you're a leader, a delegator, and a strategist. And this shift can be uncomfortable. In the early stages, founders often thrive on hands-on involvement in every area of the business, but as the business grows, this becomes unsustainable. The ability to delegate becomes paramount. But many founders struggle with this transition. They feel the need to keep their hands in every aspect of the business and can become micromanagers. This is a critical mistake. Micromanaging during the scaling phase can create bottlenecks, slow decision-making, and stifle creativity.

Hap Klopp, the founder of The North Face, famously discussed this evolution in leadership. He acknowledged that transitioning from a founder to a leader was not easy, but it was necessary for the success of the business. Klopp realized that to scale his business and ensure its long-term success, he had to let go of control and empower others to step up. This shift in mindset allowed The North Face to grow into a global brand. In fact, the ability to delegate effectively is often what separates successful entrepreneurs from those who fail during the scaling process.

Part of the leadership evolution also involves learning when to say no. As your business scales, you'll face numerous opportunities. New partnerships, big retail deals, product extensions—there will be a constant stream of potential avenues for growth. The temptation to say yes to everything is strong, especially when you're trying to take advantage of every opportunity to grow. However, not every opportunity is the right fit for your business at a given moment. Stacy Madison, the founder of Stacy's Pita Chips, had to make some tough decisions when major retailers came knocking. Instead of rushing into every opportunity, she took a more measured approach, ensuring that her company could meet the demand without sacrificing the quality or integrity of her product. Stacy's decision to prioritize sustainable growth over immediate expansion paid off, and her brand eventually became a household name.

Cash flow is another critical consideration when scaling. It's easy to think that rapid growth means you're in the clear financially, but in reality, the opposite is often true. Growth requires significant investment—whether it's in inventory, hiring, infrastructure, or marketing. As your business expands, your need for capital increases. The challenge is balancing the need for cash flow with the reality that growth itself drains your resources. Without proper financial planning and forecasting, you may find yourself in a situation where you're growing too fast but don't have the resources to sustain it. This is where financial discipline becomes crucial.

Many entrepreneurs facing these challenges consider raising capital to fund their growth. While some bootstrap their businesses and avoid outside investment, others opt to bring in investors to help fuel the next stage of expansion. However, this decision should not be taken lightly. Outside funding brings with it pressures to grow quickly and meet specific milestones. For some businesses, this can be exactly what they need to scale; for others, it can feel like a misstep. The key is understanding when outside investment is necessary and when it might do more harm than good. Not every company should aim for massive, fast-paced growth, and investors often have their own timelines and expectations that don't align with a founder's vision.

Ultimately, scaling a business is not about chasing size for the sake of size. The most successful founders understand that growth must align with their vision and values. Not all entrepreneurs aspire to build multi-million-dollar companies; some prefer to keep things small, sustainable, and manageable. Success is not measured solely by revenue or market share—it's about building a business that reflects who you are, what you stand for, and how you want your brand to grow.

The scaling phase can be incredibly rewarding, but it's also a high-stakes period in the life of a business. Some businesses emerge from scaling stronger and more resilient than ever, while others crumble under the pressure. The key to success during this phase is adaptability. The founders who make it through scaling are the ones who are able to pivot when necessary, hire the right people, maintain quality, and shift their mindset from operator to leader. It's a critical stage in the business lifecycle, and the choices you make now will shape your company's future. Growth is a double-edged sword, and it's your ability to navigate it wisely that will determine whether your business thrives or falters.

"Connect with mentors who have done what you're doing, before."

-Sophia Edelstein, Co-Founder of Pair Eyewear

Chapter 7

The Dark Side – Burnout, Failures & The Price of Success

Entrepreneurship is often painted with the brightest colors, highlighting the success stories and the shiny exits, but it's important to pull back the curtain and take a hard look at the unspoken side of the journey. The truth is that entrepreneurship, while rewarding, is an unforgiving path filled with moments of exhaustion, doubt, and a slew of failures that don't make the headlines. It's about building something from scratch, creating something that stands for more than just a business, and yet, often at a great cost. The price of success is not just in dollars—it's also in health, relationships, and, ultimately, mental resilience.

Burnout isn't just a buzzword in the startup world; it's a real threat that looms over entrepreneurs like a dark cloud. Early on, the stakes are high, and many founders find themselves working around the clock, often sacrificing sleep, personal time, and sometimes even their health just to keep the business alive. In the hustle, there's a constant pressure to meet investor expectations, stay ahead of competitors, and turn the idea into something tangible. For many, the grind feels unrelenting, and the only solution seems to be pushing harder.

That's where the myth of the "grind culture" comes in. Hustle hard, grind all day, work through the weekend—that's the mantra of many entrepreneurs. It's celebrated on social media, and it's often framed as a badge of honor. But what many fail to acknowledge is that this grind doesn't just come with a toll on productivity; it deteriorates the very things that make entrepreneurship enjoyable in the first place—creativity, decision-making, and the ability to appreciate the fruits of the labor. As founders push themselves beyond their limits, burnout sneaks in. It's a slow, insidious process, and before you know it, it can take over, turning what was once a passion into something that feels more like a burden.

Stacy Madison, the founder of Stacy's Pita Chips, experienced this firsthand. What started as a small, passionate endeavor to create a better pita chip for the world turned into a high-pressure business that required constant attention. As the demands of scaling and running a business grew, so did the toll it took on her. Stacy's experience is far from unique; many entrepreneurs hit a point where the excitement of building a brand becomes overshadowed by the never-ending cycle of stress. For Stacy, that moment came when she realized that her well-being had to come first. She stepped back, took a break, and found a new balance, even though doing so meant giving up the "hustle" mentality that's often glorified. For many founders, the question becomes: Can you build something incredible without losing yourself in the process?

Burnout in entrepreneurship isn't just a personal issue; it also impacts the business. It affects decision-making, the ability to innovate, and even the relationships within the company. But the hustle culture is so deeply ingrained that many founders wear burnout like a badge of honor, pushing through the mental and physical exhaustion because they believe it's necessary for success. The irony is that the constant grind that many entrepreneurs celebrate can eventually become their undoing. In some cases, the toll is so great that founders are forced to walk away from the very thing they worked so hard to create. The sad truth is that the culture of hustle rarely comes with the necessary conversation about the price it exacts on mental health, physical health, and relationships.

But burnout isn't the only dark side to the entrepreneurial journey. Failure, as inevitable as it is, can feel like a personal defeat. Every entrepreneur will face setbacks; it's not a matter of *if*, but *when*. A bad partnership, a failed product launch, a misstep in strategy—these moments of failure are the true tests of resilience. The difference between entrepreneurs who make it and those who don't often lies in how they handle failure. Resilience doesn't mean avoiding mistakes—it's about how you react when things go wrong.

One of the most defining aspects of successful entrepreneurs is their ability to detach from the emotional weight of failure. Failure is part of the process, and the sooner you can accept that, the faster you can pivot and learn from it. Every misstep becomes a lesson, and it's in these moments that you build the resilience that will carry you through to the next phase of your journey. The ability to view failure as a stepping stone, rather than a roadblock, is a crucial mindset shift that allows entrepreneurs to move forward, even when the odds feel stacked against them.

Joe Foster, the founder of Reebok, is a perfect example of how setbacks can be turned into opportunities for growth. From legal battles to manufacturing issues, Reebok faced a host of challenges in its early years.

Each time something went wrong, Foster refused to accept failure as the final answer. Instead, he took each setback as an opportunity to adjust, adapt, and improve. This mindset was what helped Reebok become a global brand. It wasn't just about having a great product; it was about persevering through the hard times and refusing to give up when things got tough.

But for many entrepreneurs, the financial burden is one of the most pressing struggles. The constant pressure to keep the business running—managing cash flow, meeting payroll, and ensuring the lights stay on—can be emotionally draining. In the early years, many founders forgo their own paychecks, drain their savings, or even take on personal debt just to keep the business afloat. The financial uncertainty is a major stressor that often gets overlooked in the success stories. The strain can cause anxiety, making every decision feel like it carries the weight of the world.

And yet, despite the struggle, entrepreneurs continue because they believe in what they're building. They're driven by a vision, by the belief that their work will pay off, even if the road ahead seems rocky. The problem, though, is that many founders lose sight of the fact that success isn't just about growing the business. It's about finding balance—both for themselves and for the business. The personal cost of chasing success is often not fully understood until it's too late.

Jaime Schmidt, founder of Schmidt's Naturals, has openly spoken about the emotional and mental toll of building her company. The stress of scaling, maintaining product quality, and eventually selling her brand to Unilever was immense. While Schmidt's Naturals became a household name, Jaime paid a personal price for that success. She's been transparent about how entrepreneurship took a toll on her emotional well-being. She built a successful company, but she also faced immense pressure and stress in the process. This type of honesty is rare in the entrepreneurship space, where the narrative is often skewed to focus solely on the positive.

Entrepreneurs often talk about the loneliness that comes with building a business, but it's a conversation that doesn't happen enough. Even with a dedicated team, there's a loneliness that comes from carrying the weight of responsibility. Entrepreneurs are the visionaries, the decision-makers, the ones who need to push through when others might falter. They feel the weight of their employees' expectations, their investors' demands, and their customers' trust. The burden can feel isolating, especially when there's no one else who truly understands the magnitude of the decisions being made.

This loneliness, combined with the constant pressure to succeed, leads to mental and emotional fatigue. The mental resilience required to lead a business is often underestimated. Entrepreneurs may face self-doubt, questioning whether they're truly capable of leading their company or if they're just pretending to be the leader everyone thinks they are. This internal battle can lead to imposter syndrome, a feeling that the success they've achieved isn't deserved, which can amplify stress and anxiety.

Imposter syndrome is a vicious cycle—it can make entrepreneurs question their decisions, undermine their confidence, and cause them to feel like failures, even when the external results suggest otherwise. The pressure to be perfect, to always have the answers, and to appear successful in every aspect of the business can be overwhelming. In reality, most entrepreneurs are just figuring it out as they go, and the feeling of being "out of your depth" is a shared experience, even for the most seasoned business owners.

The price of success is rarely discussed in the same breath as success itself. The mental, emotional, and physical toll of building and scaling a business can be profound. Burnout, failures, financial strain, and loneliness are the hidden costs that come with the territory. Yet, despite the hardships, entrepreneurs continue to push forward because of the love for their work, their vision, and the belief that their business will make a meaningful impact.

But there's a crucial lesson to learn: success isn't just about building a business—it's about building a life that can sustain that business. Entrepreneurs who prioritize balance, take care of their mental health, and find ways to manage stress are the ones who endure. They learn how to pace themselves, delegate effectively, and, perhaps most importantly, take care of themselves, so they can continue the long, hard journey. Entrepreneurship is a marathon, not a sprint. And those who make it through to the other side are the ones who've learned how to navigate the dark side of entrepreneurship without losing themselves in the process.

"When you think you're dreaming big, dream bigger."

-Dr. Jonathan B. Levine, Founder of JBL NYC

Chapter 8

The Pivot – Adapting When Things Go Wrong

Adapting in business isn't just a skill—it's survival. The market isn't stagnant, and neither is consumer behavior. People's needs change, industries shift, new competitors emerge, and sometimes, the idea that once seemed like a sure thing simply stops working. The founders who build lasting companies aren't just those with the best initial ideas. They're the ones who recognize when something isn't working, when the market is telling them to change course, and when an opportunity is bigger than the one they originally envisioned.

Every entrepreneur starts with a vision, but the ones who succeed aren't necessarily the ones who stick to it no matter what. They're the ones who adapt. The ones who realize that the original idea isn't what matters most—what matters is solving a real problem in a way people are willing to pay for. Pivots aren't a sign of failure. They're a sign of listening, evolving, and making the necessary moves to keep a business relevant.

One of the best examples of this is Stacy Madison. She never set out to start a snack company. She ran a food cart in Boston, making healthy sandwiches for professionals on their lunch breaks. As a way to make use of extra bread, she started baking pita chips and handing them out as free samples to customers waiting in line. They weren't meant to be a product—just something to keep people happy while they waited. But the response was undeniable. People weren't just enjoying them; they were asking to buy them.

That's where a lot of founders miss their moment. They get so attached to the business they originally set out to build that they ignore what the market is telling them. Stacy could have dismissed the chips as a side product and stayed focused on her sandwich business. But she didn't. She paid attention to demand, saw where the real opportunity was, and pivoted. That shift turned a small side experiment into one of the biggest snack brands in the country.

The same principle applies across industries. The best founders are constantly scanning for signals. What are customers saying? Where is the friction? What is selling, and what isn't? Pivoting isn't about chasing trends or making changes just for the sake of it—it's about recognizing when something isn't working as well as it could be and having the courage to shift directions. It's about putting aside ego and being willing to admit that a different approach might be better than the one you originally envisioned.

Jaime Schmidt, the founder of Schmidt's Naturals, experienced this firsthand. When she started making natural deodorant, it wasn't because she had plans to build a multimillion-dollar company. She was just looking for a healthier alternative for her family. But when she started selling her homemade deodorant at local markets, she realized there was a massive gap in the market. People wanted natural products that actually worked. Instead of treating her deodorant as just another homemade good, she leaned into the movement toward clean personal care, refining her branding and expanding her product line. That pivot—seeing the bigger opportunity beyond just deodorant—turned Schmidt's Naturals into a company that eventually sold to Unilever.

Pivots don't always mean completely changing the business. Sometimes, it's just a small but critical shift—adjusting messaging, pricing, or distribution. A great example of this is HexClad. When they first launched, their hybrid cookware was revolutionary—combining the best of nonstick and stainless steel. But their early messaging wasn't landing. People didn't fully understand what made the product different. Instead of scrapping the idea, they refined their approach, simplifying the way they explained the benefits and focusing their marketing efforts on a clearer value proposition. That subtle shift made all the difference, helping HexClad carve out a dominant space in the cookware industry.

The hardest part of pivoting is knowing when it's necessary. Many founders struggle to separate short-term struggles from long-term viability. Every business has slow sales periods, unexpected challenges, and roadblocks that don't necessarily mean the entire model is broken. The key is identifying whether the problem is something that can be fixed with better execution or whether the market itself is telling you to change course.

There's a fine line between persistence and stubbornness, and too many founders fall on the wrong side of it. They keep pushing a product that isn't selling, convinced they just need more time, better marketing, or more funding to make it work. But time doesn't fix a flawed idea. Listening to customers does. If people aren't buying, if retention is low, if the market isn't responding, something needs to change. The best founders don't just push harder—they push smarter. They analyze what's working, cut what isn't, and adapt before it's too late.

This doesn't mean reacting to every bump in the road with a total overhaul. Some businesses pivot too often, chasing every new idea without giving anything a chance to gain traction. That's just as dangerous as not pivoting at all. The difference is in the data. Is the market actually telling you something isn't working, or are you just getting impatient? Are you pivoting because the business isn't sustainable, or are you just uncomfortable with how long success takes?

A well-executed pivot isn't just about survival—it's often the thing that unlocks the true potential of a business. Some of the most successful companies in the world look nothing like they did when they started. YouTube began as a dating site before realizing that video-sharing was the real opportunity. Slack started as a gaming company but pivoted into workplace communication when they saw that their internal chat tool had more potential than the game itself. Instagram originally launched as a location-based check-in app before realizing that users were far more interested in the photo-sharing feature.

Pivots can be minor course corrections or major overhauls. What matters is the ability to recognize when a change is necessary and act decisively. A slow pivot is often just as bad as no pivot at all. Entrepreneurs who hesitate, who second-guess themselves, who spend too much time overanalyzing instead of executing, often miss their window. The market moves fast, and if you're not willing to adapt, someone else will.

Founders who successfully pivot often share a few key traits. They listen more than they talk. They watch how customers behave instead of just assuming they know what people want. They're flexible without being directionless, knowing when to adjust without constantly second-guessing their strategy. They embrace change rather than fear it, understanding that no company follows a straight path.

Adaptation is one of the most underrated skills in entrepreneurship. It's easy to think that the best founders are just the ones with the biggest vision, but that's not the full story. The ones who last aren't necessarily the ones with the best ideas from day one. They're the ones who learn the fastest, pivot when necessary, and aren't afraid to evolve.

The harsh reality is that no business follows a straight path. Even the most successful companies have had to shift, tweak, and sometimes completely reinvent themselves to stay relevant. The ones that survive aren't always the ones that started with the best plan. They're the ones that refused to stay stuck. The ones that had the humility to admit when something wasn't working and the courage to make the change.

Pivoting isn't about giving up on a vision. It's about reshaping that vision into something that actually works. The market doesn't care about what you *thought* was a great idea. It cares about what it *needs*. The founders who build lasting businesses are the ones who aren't afraid to listen.

"Make sure you're all ears when opportunities to learn are there."

-Kevin McCray, Founder of Kevin's Natural Foods

Chapter 9

The Power of Brand – How Great Companies Build Loyalty

Building a strong product is essential, but in today's crowded marketplace, a great product alone isn't enough. The brands that stand the test of time go beyond transactions. They create emotional connections with their customers, turning one-time buyers into lifelong advocates. A powerful brand fosters loyalty, drives word-of-mouth marketing, and ultimately becomes the reason customers choose one company over another. The most successful companies understand that they are not just selling a product or a service—they are selling an identity, a belief system, and a story that resonates with people on a deeper level. When customers feel an emotional connection to a brand, they aren't just purchasing a product, they are aligning themselves with a set of values that reflect their own. They aren't just buying what the company sells; they are buying into why the company exists in the first place.

A brand is more than a logo or a slogan—it's the story, values, and personality that shape how people perceive a business. The best brands make customers feel something. They build trust, inspire community, and communicate a purpose beyond just selling a product. They make consumers believe in something bigger than the product itself. Hap Klopp, who took The North Face from a small outdoor gear shop to a globally recognized brand, understood this deeply. He wasn't just selling jackets and backpacks—he was selling adventure, resilience, and a deep respect for the outdoors. Everything about the brand, from its marketing campaigns to its product design, reinforced the idea that The North Face wasn't just about clothing; it was about a lifestyle. That emotional connection turned customers into lifelong brand advocates who didn't just buy gear—they aligned themselves with an identity of exploration and durability. A brand's identity becomes a competitive advantage when it connects deeply with its customers' values. That connection fosters a loyalty that withstands price competition and industry trends. When a brand is built on a solid foundation, customers return not just because they need a product, but because they feel a sense of belonging.

But building a brand with that level of connection doesn't happen overnight. It requires clarity, authenticity, and consistency at every touchpoint. Companies that fail to establish a strong brand identity struggle to differentiate themselves, making it easy for competitors to step in and take their place. Authenticity is one of the most valuable aspects of branding. Consumers today are savvier than ever. They can tell when a brand is being disingenuous or jumping on a trend just to stay relevant. Brands that succeed long-term don't just market to their audience—they listen to them and reflect their values.

Jaime Schmidt, the founder of Schmidt's Naturals, never set out to create a mass-market personal care brand. She was simply making deodorant in her kitchen that she felt was safer for her family. When she started selling her product at local farmers' markets, she didn't have a massive branding strategy—what she had was authenticity. She was creating a product for people like her, and that resonated. As her company grew, she never lost that grassroots connection with her customers. Even after expanding into major retailers and eventually selling to Unilever, she ensured that the brand remained committed to transparency and natural ingredients. Customers trusted Schmidt's Naturals because they knew exactly what they were getting—no gimmicks, no shortcuts, just a quality product with a clear purpose.

That trust is what makes branding so powerful. When customers believe in a brand, they don't just buy its products; they advocate for it. They tell their friends. They defend it online. They wear it proudly. That's why some brands succeed while others disappear—because the best brands don't just create products, they create movements. Some brands succeed because they position themselves as aspirational. Customers don't just buy the product—they buy into an exclusive lifestyle. Brands like Apple, Tesla, and Rolex understand that people want to feel like they're part of something elite.

HexClad, the hybrid cookware company, took this approach in an industry that isn't typically known for branding. Instead of competing on price, HexClad positioned itself as the premium choice—an investment in better cooking. Their marketing wasn't about selling pans; it was about selling the idea that you could cook like a professional. By elevating the perception of their cookware, they built a loyal customer base that was willing to pay a premium. Their customers weren't just buying HexClad because it worked; they were buying it because of what it represented—quality, innovation, and a professional-grade experience.

Luxury brands and premium-positioned brands often use scarcity and high-end messaging to elevate their desirability. They don't compete on features alone—they compete on image. And when a company carefully crafts its image and sticks to its values, customers willingly pay a premium because they're not just buying a product—they're buying a piece of the brand's story. But no matter the industry, the most effective brands all share one common trait: they understand the power of storytelling. People remember stories more than they remember facts. The best brands use storytelling to humanize their business and build a deeper emotional connection with customers. Whether it's the founder's origin story, a customer's experience, or an inside look at the production process, strong narratives create engagement and inspire loyalty.

Nike has mastered this. Their marketing isn't about selling shoes—it's about selling perseverance, ambition, and the relentless pursuit of greatness. They don't just showcase athletes; they highlight the struggles and triumphs that make those athletes human. That storytelling is what makes customers feel something. It's what makes people feel like they are part of something bigger. Smaller brands can learn from this. A compelling brand story can turn a small business into a movement. Customers don't just buy products; they buy into the journey, mission, and impact that a brand represents.

The key is authenticity—stories must be real, compelling, and rooted in the brand's actual values.

The brands that fail are often the ones that lack a clear identity. Companies that chase trends without a strong foundation struggle to build lasting customer relationships. The best brands stay consistent in their messaging, visuals, and values. No matter how much they grow, their customers always recognize what they stand for. Brand loyalty is built through repetition and trust. A brand must communicate its values consistently across all touchpoints—from packaging to customer service to social media. If a company's marketing says one thing, but its customer experience delivers another, trust erodes quickly. Successful brands ensure that every interaction reinforces the same message and mission. But great branding goes beyond marketing—it builds community.

The strongest brands don't just have customers; they have communities. When people feel like they belong to something, they naturally become brand advocates. They talk about it, recommend it, and defend it. Patagonia is a perfect example of this. They aren't just an outdoor brand; they're an environmental movement. Customers don't just buy Patagonia products—they align themselves with Patagonia's mission. By taking a stand on issues that matter to their audience, Patagonia has built one of the most loyal customer bases in the world. That's the ultimate power of branding. It turns customers into advocates, businesses into movements, and products into something more than just items to be purchased.

The brands that last are the ones with a purpose beyond profit. They stand for something meaningful, and customers recognize that. Whether it's sustainability, craftsmanship, innovation, or social impact, brands that lead with purpose stand out in a crowded market. A great brand is more than a business—it's a relationship. It's the reason why customers choose one company over another, even when the products are similar. It's what turns buyers into lifelong fans who continue to support the business for years, not just because of what they sell, but because of what they represent.

In a world where consumers have endless options, a strong brand is what makes a business unforgettable. It's not just about having a recognizable name or a great product—it's about making people feel something, about giving them a reason to choose you over everyone else. The businesses that understand this don't just build companies. They build legacies.

"You're going to have all kinds of challenges that you never imagined, being an entrepreneur. It's all about perseverance."

-Bill Phelps, Co-Founder of Wetzel's Pretzels, CEO of Dave's Hot Chicken

Chapter 10

Marketing That Works – Strategies for Growth

Creating a great product is only half the battle. Getting people to care about it, talk about it, and ultimately buy it is what separates successful brands from those that fade into obscurity. Marketing isn't just about spending money on ads. The best founders understand how to blend organic growth strategies, paid advertising, influencer collaborations, and viral tactics into a cohesive plan that builds long-term brand equity. In a world where attention is the most valuable currency, the brands that know how to command it, keep it, and turn it into loyalty are the ones that thrive.

For startups, organic marketing is often the first step. Without a big budget, early-stage companies rely on social media, search engine optimization, and email marketing to create awareness. Social media, especially platforms like Instagram, TikTok, and YouTube, has given brands an unprecedented opportunity to connect directly with their audience. Instead of relying on traditional advertising, smart entrepreneurs engage their followers with valuable content, behind-the-scenes access, and authentic storytelling. Founders who personally interact with their audience—responding to comments, showing product development, and building a genuine community—often see their brands grow organically through word-of-mouth. Consumers trust people more than they trust brands, and when a founder is actively involved in the conversation, the brand feels more human. The companies that win aren't just the ones that push the hardest—they're the ones that listen the most.

SEO plays a critical role in sustainable growth. Ranking highly on Google for relevant search terms allows brands to attract customers without relying on continuous ad spending. Companies that invest in quality blog content, optimize their websites, and earn backlinks from reputable sources gain long-term traction that compounds over time. Unlike social media, where algorithms can change overnight, a strong search presence provides consistent traffic for years. But SEO isn't about keyword stuffing or gaming the system—it's about creating genuinely helpful content that answers customer questions. The brands that succeed in search are the ones that position themselves as industry leaders, constantly providing value before asking for a sale.

Email marketing is another overlooked but highly effective channel. Unlike social platforms where algorithms control visibility, email lists give businesses direct access to their customers. Brands that build trust through email—sending valuable content instead of just promotional blasts—develop a loyal customer base that continues to engage with their products over time. A strong email strategy isn't about sending as many emails as possible; it's about sending the right emails to the right people at the right time. The best companies use segmentation, automation, and personalization to make their email marketing feel less like spam and more like a direct conversation.

While organic strategies lay the foundation, paid advertising is what accelerates growth. Facebook and Instagram ads remain dominant in e-commerce and direct-to-consumer marketing, though rising costs make efficiency more important than ever. The most successful brands don't just throw money at ads; they rigorously test creatives, headlines, and targeting to maximize returns. A winning ad today might be outdated in a month, which is why constant iteration is crucial. TikTok advertising has emerged as a major force, particularly for younger audiences. Unlike traditional platforms, TikTok's algorithm favors discovery, making it easier for brands to gain traction. The key to success isn't polished, corporate-style ads—it's content that feels native to the platform. Brands that embrace a more casual, relatable approach tend to see better results.

Google Ads are another powerful tool, particularly for businesses that rely on search intent. While social media ads target users who may not have been looking for a product, Google Ads capture customers actively searching for solutions. A well-optimized Google campaign ensures that when someone types in a problem, a brand's product is the answer. Retargeting ads, which show products to users who have visited a website but didn't purchase, are one of the highest-ROI advertising strategies. Most customers don't buy on their first visit, so keeping a product in front of them across different platforms significantly increases conversions.

Influencer marketing has become a critical component of modern brand growth. The most effective campaigns aren't with the biggest influencers but with the most engaged ones. Micro-influencers, those with smaller but highly dedicated followings, often deliver better results than celebrities because their audience trusts them. Smart brands focus on long-term partnerships rather than one-off sponsored posts. When influencers genuinely love a product and integrate it into their content consistently, it feels more authentic, leading to stronger conversion rates. The key is finding influencers whose audiences overlap with your target customers—not just chasing the biggest names.

Affiliate marketing takes influencer partnerships a step further by aligning incentives. Instead of paying a flat fee for a post, brands offer influencers a commission for each sale they generate. This performance-based model ensures that brands only pay for actual results, making it a cost-effective way to scale. Some of the most successful companies have built entire businesses through affiliate partnerships, leveraging creators as an extended salesforce without traditional ad spend.

Viral marketing remains one of the most unpredictable yet powerful ways to grow. Word-of-mouth remains one of the strongest drivers of consumer behavior, and brands that create shareable moments often experience exponential growth. Encouraging user-generated content—where customers create videos, testimonials, and social posts about a product—turns them into brand ambassadors. When potential buyers see real people talking about a product in an organic way, they're far more likely to trust and engage with it. Some brands engineer virality through PR stunts, collaborations, or bold marketing moves. Whether it's launching an unexpected product, tapping into a cultural moment, or taking a public stand on an issue, well-executed stunts generate massive attention at a fraction of the cost of traditional advertising.

Referrals are another underutilized but highly effective marketing strategy. The best customers are the ones who bring in more customers. Many successful brands implement referral programs that incentivize existing customers to share a product with their friends in exchange for discounts, exclusive perks, or other rewards. This taps into the basic psychology that people trust recommendations from those they know far more than they trust ads. A well-structured referral program can turn an initial wave of customers into a self-sustaining engine of growth.

The future of marketing is constantly shifting, but one trend is clear—brands must own their audience. Privacy regulations and changes in online advertising make first-party data more valuable than ever. Businesses that build direct relationships through email, SMS, and community engagement will be in the strongest position to navigate these shifts. Personalization will also continue to be a major factor. Customers expect brands to understand their preferences, and those that tailor experiences—whether through AI-driven recommendations or segmented email campaigns—will outperform those that use a generic approach.

Storytelling remains at the core of every effective marketing strategy. The brands that stand out are the ones that tell compelling stories—whether through their origin, their mission, or the people who use their products. People don't remember facts; they remember emotions. Companies that can make customers feel something—whether it's nostalgia, excitement, or inspiration—build brands that last.

No single marketing strategy guarantees success. The most resilient brands diversify their efforts, combining organic and paid strategies, leveraging storytelling, and constantly adapting to new trends. The key is iteration. What works today might not work a year from now, and businesses that stay flexible, test different approaches, and focus on building relationships rather than just transactions will be the ones that last. The best marketing isn't just about getting attention—it's about earning trust, creating demand, and turning customers into a community that continues to grow long after the first sale.

"You don't have to do it alone. Find a network who can help you."

-Kyle Widrick, Founder of Win Brands Group

Chapter 11

Distribution & Partnerships – Getting in Front of the Right Customers

A great product and strong brand mean nothing if they don't reach the right customers. Distribution is often an afterthought for new entrepreneurs, but it is one of the most critical aspects of a business. A company can have the best product in the world, but if it isn't available where customers expect to find it, growth will stall. The most successful founders don't just rely on one distribution channel—they build a mix of direct sales, retail partnerships, online marketplaces, and strategic collaborations to maximize their reach while staying in control of their brand. The key to winning in distribution is being intentional. Expanding too fast into the wrong channels can dilute brand equity, strain supply chains, and lead to cash flow problems that can cripple a business. On the other hand, waiting too long to scale distribution can cause a brand to miss its moment, allowing competitors to establish dominance in key retail spaces or online marketplaces.

Direct-to-consumer (DTC) brands exploded in the 2010s, thanks to social media marketing and lower barriers to entry. By selling directly through their websites, brands like Warby Parker, Allbirds, and Glossier were able to bypass traditional retail markups and build direct relationships with customers. This allowed them to own customer data, optimize marketing campaigns, and create a seamless brand experience without interference from third-party retailers. However, as competition increased and digital advertising costs skyrocketed, many DTC companies realized they couldn't rely solely on this model. Expanding into retail and marketplaces like Amazon became necessary to scale profitably. What worked in the early DTC era—leaning heavily on Facebook and Instagram ads—stopped being cost-effective as customer acquisition costs soared. Many brands that initially prided themselves on being "online-only" had to rethink their strategies.

The key to making DTC work long-term is owning customer data. Unlike retail or wholesale, where brands don't control the end customer relationship, selling directly allows companies to collect valuable insights, personalize marketing efforts, and build loyalty programs that drive repeat purchases. Brands that succeed in DTC long-term go beyond just selling a product—they create an ecosystem that makes customers want to engage directly with them rather than through third-party retailers. Subscription models, exclusive online-only product drops, and strong content strategies help brands build deeper relationships with their audiences, reducing reliance on paid advertising. The most effective DTC brands think about lifetime value, not just customer acquisition. They understand that the first purchase is just the beginning, and they optimize every part of the experience to keep customers coming back.

Wholesale and retail partnerships remain powerful distribution channels, but they require careful planning. Brands that rush into big-box retail often struggle with pricing, inventory demands, and brand positioning. Retailers control shelf space, pricing strategies, and promotional placements, which can put pressure on brands to discount their products or compete directly with private-label alternatives. One example of a brand that executed retail expansion well is Schmidt's Naturals. Founder Jaime Schmidt started selling her natural deodorant at farmers' markets before scaling into Whole Foods. By proving demand in small, niche retailers first, she was able to negotiate better terms when larger retailers showed interest. This gradual, controlled approach allowed her to maintain pricing integrity and ensure the brand didn't get lost on crowded shelves. Many brands that fail in retail expansion do so because they overextend too quickly, signing deals with national chains before they fully understand what works in physical retail. The brands that win are the ones that treat retail as a strategic play, not just a volume game.

Amazon is a distribution powerhouse, but it comes with risks. Many brands see Amazon as an unavoidable sales channel, but the platform's control over pricing and customer data can make it a double-edged sword. Reebok, for example, initially hesitated to sell on Amazon due to concerns over discounting and brand dilution. However, realizing the platform's reach, they implemented a selective distribution strategy, selling only specific product lines while keeping premium collections exclusive to their website and retail partners. This allowed them to tap into Amazon's vast customer base without fully surrendering control. Brands that use Amazon strategically rather than as their primary channel tend to see the best results. The biggest mistake brands make with Amazon is assuming it's purely an e-commerce play. It's also a discovery engine. Many consumers start their product searches on Amazon, and even if they don't buy there, they use it for research before purchasing directly from a brand's website or a physical store. Smart brands recognize this and optimize their Amazon presence with strong product pages, compelling A+ content, and customer reviews while ensuring they're not overly reliant on the platform for sales.

Subscription models have emerged as a unique distribution strategy, creating predictable revenue streams and deeper customer relationships. Companies like Dollar Shave Club and Birchbox pioneered this model, leveraging convenience and exclusivity to keep customers engaged long-term. The biggest advantage of a subscription model is recurring revenue, which smooths out cash flow and reduces dependence on constant customer acquisition. However, for subscription-based brands, retention is just as important as acquisition. Those that fail to continuously add value—whether through personalized experiences, exclusive content, or surprise elements—struggle to keep customers subscribed beyond the initial novelty. Many subscription companies that once thrived have since collapsed because they underestimated how hard it is to maintain excitement over time. The best subscription brands evolve. They introduce new products, offer flexibility in billing and shipments, and ensure customers never feel trapped in a subscription they no longer want.

Partnerships can be a game-changer for distribution. Strategic collaborations allow brands to tap into new audiences without the costs of traditional advertising.

One of the best examples of a partnership-driven growth strategy is Nike and Apple. Their collaboration on the Nike+ product line combined Nike's brand credibility in fitness with Apple's technological expertise, creating a seamless experience for consumers. Smaller brands can adopt similar tactics by partnering with complementary companies that share their target audience. For example, a premium coffee brand could partner with a high-end kitchenware company to co-market products through bundled deals or exclusive content. Partnerships aren't just about slapping two logos together—they work best when they create a better experience for the customer than either brand could provide on its own.

Another growing trend in distribution is experiential retail. Pop-up shops, brand activations, and limited-time retail partnerships create urgency and excitement around a product. DTC brands that started online, like Glossier and Warby Parker, have leveraged experiential retail to deepen relationships with customers in physical spaces without committing to traditional retail leases. These activations not only generate sales but also serve as powerful brand-building moments.

When choosing distribution channels, brands must consider factors like customer experience, control over pricing, and scalability. The biggest mistake entrepreneurs make is assuming more distribution automatically equals more sales. The wrong retail partnership, an unoptimized Amazon presence, or an underwhelming direct-to-consumer strategy can do more harm than good. A strong omnichannel approach blends direct sales, retail, marketplace, and partnership strategies to reach customers where they naturally shop while maintaining brand integrity. Brands that win in distribution are those that remain flexible, experiment with different channels, and optimize based on real data rather than assumptions.

At the end of the day, the best distribution strategy is the one that makes it easiest for customers to buy. Whether through a brand's website, a major retailer, or a subscription model, the key is reducing friction in the purchasing process. The businesses that scale the fastest are the ones that don't force customers to adapt to their model—instead, they meet customers where they already are. Whether through direct-to-consumer, retail, marketplaces, or partnerships, successful founders understand that distribution isn't just about getting products into more places—it's about getting them into the *right* places. The companies that get this right don't just sell more—they build lasting, scalable brands that stand the test of time.

"Challenge your assumptions across everything and keep showing up."

-Jaime Schmidt, Founder of Schmidt's Naturals

Chapter 12

Customer Experience – Why It Matters More Than Anything Else

A great product may bring a customer in once, but a great experience keeps them coming back. The best brands aren't just selling products—they're creating memorable interactions that turn first-time buyers into lifelong advocates. Customer experience isn't just about having a friendly support team; it's woven into every part of a business, from the way products are designed to how orders are packaged and the emotions people feel when interacting with the brand. A product can be replicated. A price can be undercut. But a world-class customer experience is nearly impossible to compete with, and it's what separates good businesses from legendary ones.

Many startups obsess over acquiring new customers but neglect what happens after the purchase. This is a critical mistake. The brands that scale successfully understand that retaining an existing customer is far more cost-effective than acquiring a new one. Every transaction is an opportunity to create a repeat customer, and brands that invest in post-purchase relationships build trust and fuel word-of-mouth marketing, which often becomes the strongest driver of long-term growth. When customers feel appreciated and valued, they return—and, more importantly, they tell others.

Stacy Madison, founder of Stacy's Pita Chips, understood this well. She started her business by handing out samples from a food cart, creating a personal connection with customers before her brand ever hit store shelves. Those early days built her understanding of how to make people feel connected to a product beyond just its taste. Even as the company scaled into mass distribution, she kept that personalized touch in mind—prioritizing product quality, engaging with customers, and ensuring that the experience of buying Stacy's Pita Chips felt just as personal as those early days. That attention to customer experience helped transform her brand from a small snack business into a nationally recognized name. She never forgot that customers weren't just buying chips—they were buying into a brand they trusted, one that had treated them well from the beginning.

HexClad, the high-performance cookware brand, also leveraged customer experience as a growth strategy. From the start, founder Daniel Winer knew that customer satisfaction wasn't just about the quality of the pans but the entire purchasing process. That's why HexClad invested in high-end packaging that made unboxing feel premium, and they built a dedicated customer service team to personally handle every inquiry. The moment a customer received their cookware, they felt like they had purchased something of lasting value. By making the experience as seamless as possible—from product education to after-purchase support—HexClad turned customers into brand advocates who not only returned but also recommended the cookware to friends and family. This wasn't just a product—it was an experience, and that made all the difference.

Customer experience isn't just about service—it extends to how a brand makes people feel at every touchpoint. Joe Foster, the founder of Reebok, built a sports brand that wasn't just about footwear; it was about belonging to a movement. Reebok's early growth wasn't just due to product innovation; it was about the emotional connection customers felt when they put on the shoes. From professional athletes to everyday customers, Reebok created a brand that made people feel empowered and valued. That sense of connection fostered a strong emotional bond between the company and its customers, leading to lifelong loyalty. When people buy into a brand at an emotional level, price and competition become secondary. They aren't just wearing a pair of sneakers—they're wearing something that represents their values, their aspirations, and their lifestyle.

Chuck Surack, the founder of Sweetwater, took customer experience to an entirely different level. His philosophy of "always do the right thing" became the guiding principle of the company, and it was reflected in every interaction with customers. From offering free technical support for life to personally checking in on buyers long after their purchase, Sweetwater built an unparalleled reputation in the music industry. The company didn't just sell instruments and gear—it created an experience that made customers feel valued and respected. That level of service built loyalty that couldn't be replicated with marketing tactics alone. The most effective growth strategies aren't gimmicks—they're built on real relationships.

Another critical aspect of customer experience is response time. Customers today expect immediate support, and brands that master fast, thoughtful communication build trust. Companies that force customers through endless automated systems or long wait times often see negative reviews that damage their reputation. A slow response feels like a lack of care, and in a world where consumers have more choices than ever, they will move on without hesitation. The brands that thrive are those that treat customer interactions as an opportunity to build relationships, not just resolve issues. The companies that win are the ones that make a customer feel heard and valued, not just another ticket in a support queue.

Loyalty programs and exclusive perks can also enhance customer experience. Instead of treating purchases as one-off transactions, brands that create ongoing engagement keep customers coming back. Subscription models, VIP programs, and personalized recommendations based on past purchases are all ways to make customers feel valued beyond the initial sale. When a brand recognizes a returning customer and offers them something tailored to their preferences, it reinforces their decision to stay loyal. Companies that succeed at this aren't just selling products—they're building communities. When a brand feels like a membership rather than just a store, customers feel a deeper connection.

Measuring customer satisfaction is key to maintaining a high-level experience. Founders who are serious about growth track feedback relentlessly, using post-purchase surveys, Net Promoter Scores (NPS), and direct conversations to understand how customers truly feel. The most successful entrepreneurs don't assume they're delivering a great experience—they continuously refine it based on real data and customer insights. It's easy to believe that your product and service are exceptional, but if the customer experience doesn't match, that disconnect will eventually show in retention rates and referrals. The brands that last are the ones that make adjustments based on what their customers actually want, not just what they assume will work.

Creating an unforgettable customer experience goes beyond just good service—it's about making every interaction feel intentional. From packaging to follow-ups to the way a company handles mistakes, every detail matters. A customer who has a great experience not only buys again but becomes a brand advocate. A customer who has a bad experience may never return—and worse, they may share that negative experience with others. The cost of a lost customer is far higher than the cost of delivering great service in the first place.

The brands that win don't just sell—they delight, surprise, and exceed expectations at every turn. They don't just think about transactions; they think about relationships. The best marketing in the world can't replace a genuinely great experience, and companies that prioritize customer experience over short-term sales tactics build loyalty, create word-of-mouth growth, and ultimately stand the test of time. The businesses that scale are the ones that know that every customer interaction is a chance to create a fan, not just a buyer. They don't treat customer experience as a department—they treat it as the foundation of everything they do.

"Go into business expecting a pandemic."

-Stacy Madison, Founder of Stacy's Pita Chips

Chapter 13

Digital vs. Physical – Navigating E-Commerce & Retail

For decades, physical retail dominated. If you wanted to sell a product, you had to fight for shelf space, build relationships with buyers, and convince retailers that your product deserved a place next to legacy brands. The barriers to entry were high, and success depended largely on the ability to navigate the complexities of wholesale distribution and retail partnerships. Then, the internet changed everything. Suddenly, founders could bypass traditional gatekeepers and sell directly to consumers, cutting out the middleman and retaining full control over their brand. This shift sparked the rise of the direct-to-consumer (DTC) movement, allowing startups to scale without the overhead of brick-and-mortar stores. It gave birth to an era where companies could launch from a laptop, use digital marketing to build an audience, and ship directly to customers with minimal infrastructure.

But the reality today isn't as simple as choosing between online and physical retail—successful brands often blend both. The early DTC boom made it seem like physical retail was dead, but the brands that have endured are those that recognized the limitations of a digital-only approach. They understood that while e-commerce offered reach and efficiency, retail still played an irreplaceable role in customer trust, product discovery, and brand longevity. The idea that one model would completely replace the other was flawed from the start. Instead, the most resilient brands saw digital and physical as complementary forces rather than opposing ones.

Digital-first brands exploded in the 2010s, leveraging social media and data-driven marketing to reach customers faster and more efficiently than traditional retail ever allowed. Companies like Warby Parker and Casper built their businesses online before ever opening physical locations. The appeal of DTC was obvious: higher margins, complete control over branding, and direct access to customer data. Rather than relying on third-party retailers, these companies could craft their own customer journey, experiment with messaging in real-time, and refine their sales funnel based on direct consumer feedback. It was a game-changer, making it possible for startups to compete with established brands on a level playing field.

However, as digital ad costs skyrocketed and competition intensified, many e-commerce brands realized that scaling purely online wasn't as easy—or as profitable—as they once thought. Facebook and Google ads, once a goldmine for cost-effective customer acquisition, became increasingly expensive as more brands flooded the market. Customer acquisition costs (CAC) soared, and the economics of DTC started to break down for companies that lacked deep pockets or a strong organic brand presence. Brands that relied too heavily on digital advertising found themselves in a precarious position, forced to either raise prices, find alternative marketing channels, or expand into new distribution models.

At the same time, return rates for online purchases—especially in industries like apparel and footwear—became a major issue, eating into profits and creating logistical headaches. Unlike physical retail, where customers could try before they buy, e-commerce had to deal with the reality that many purchases resulted in returns, often due to sizing issues or unmet expectations. This added another layer of complexity to scaling online businesses, forcing brands to rethink their strategies. The brands that had built themselves entirely on digital marketing found themselves facing a new challenge: how to keep growing in a world where online attention was getting more expensive by the day.

The reality is that digital and physical retail each have their strengths and weaknesses. Online brands benefit from global reach, lower overhead, and the ability to experiment with marketing in real-time. But they also face challenges: customer acquisition costs are high, return rates can be brutal, and the lack of in-person experiences makes it harder to create brand stickiness. Physical retail, on the other hand, offers credibility, instant customer trust, and a tangible experience that e-commerce simply can't replicate. The ability to see, touch, and try a product before buying reduces uncertainty and leads to higher conversion rates. It's why, despite the rise of e-commerce, physical retail still accounts for the majority of global retail sales. Consumers may browse online, but many still prefer the reassurance of an in-store purchase.

Joe Foster, founder of Reebok, understood the power of both worlds before it was trendy to do so. Reebok built its name in traditional retail and dominated athletic stores, but the rise of digital commerce forced the company to adapt. Rather than resisting change, they embraced e-commerce as a way to deepen their relationship with customers, using online channels not just to sell, but to tell their story directly. By combining traditional retail partnerships with an expanding online presence, Reebok maintained its legacy while staying relevant in the digital age. Many heritage brands struggled to make this transition, but those that did it successfully, like Reebok, recognized that digital wasn't a replacement for physical retail—it was an extension of it.

For newer brands, the question isn't whether to sell online or in stores—it's how to balance both. Many startups begin with a DTC approach, using digital sales to validate demand before expanding into retail. Stacy Madison did this with Stacy's Pita Chips, building an audience locally before scaling into grocery chains. By proving demand early, she was able to negotiate better terms when major retailers took interest. Today, brands looking to follow a similar path often use online sales as a testing ground before making the leap into wholesale or opening their own stores. Rather than betting everything on retail partnerships from day one, they leverage digital to create momentum, using customer data to refine their positioning before engaging with large distributors.

There's also a growing trend of e-commerce brands opening physical locations—not necessarily as traditional retail stores, but as brand experiences. Companies like Glossier and Allbirds launched pop-up shops and flagship stores that serve as immersive brand environments rather than just sales channels. These spaces allow customers to interact with products in a way that digital-only businesses can't provide, while still driving online sales through in-store experiences. Glossier, for example, used its stores not just for sales, but for content creation—encouraging visitors to share their experience on social media, effectively turning their physical spaces into marketing engines. This hybrid approach allows brands to capture the best of both worlds: the reach and efficiency of digital with the trust and engagement of physical retail.

Wholesale partnerships remain a powerful distribution strategy, but they require careful execution. Selling through third-party retailers can provide massive exposure, but it often comes at the cost of control. Jaime Schmidt of Schmidt's Naturals experienced this when expanding from small independent shops to major retailers like Target and Walmart. While the partnerships introduced her brand to millions of new customers, they also meant adjusting pricing structures, meeting large-scale production demands, and maintaining brand consistency across multiple sales channels. Founders who go the wholesale route must ensure they don't compromise their brand in the process. Many brands have lost their positioning by expanding too quickly into big-box retail, only to find that their margins were squeezed and their products were treated as commodities rather than premium offerings.

At the same time, some businesses are proving that a digital-first approach can be just as powerful as traditional retail—if executed correctly. HexClad, for instance, grew almost entirely online before expanding into select retailers. The company focused on direct customer relationships, using digital marketing to tell its brand story and build trust before making the jump into wholesale. By ensuring that customers already recognized and valued the brand before seeing it on store shelves, HexClad maintained pricing power and brand authority. Unlike brands that rely solely on retail partnerships to establish themselves, HexClad used digital as its primary growth engine, allowing them to control their margins and scale on their own terms.

Ultimately, the most successful brands don't see digital and physical retail as competing forces. Instead, they use both strategically. Some customers prefer the convenience of online shopping, while others want the reassurance of an in-person experience. The key is meeting customers where they are while maintaining control over the brand's positioning. Brands that master this balance don't just survive—they dominate.

The future of retail isn't about choosing one model over the other—it's about building a business that thrives in both. Digital is essential for brand awareness, customer acquisition, and direct relationships, while physical retail provides trust, credibility, and a tangible experience that keeps customers engaged. The best companies aren't asking whether they should be online or in stores—they're figuring out how to integrate both in a way that strengthens their brand, improves customer experience, and drives long-term growth. Brands that succeed in this new era of commerce are the ones that understand the importance of flexibility—those that experiment, iterate, and adapt based on how consumers actually shop, rather than sticking to outdated assumptions about retail. The companies that win won't be the ones that resist change. They'll be the ones that embrace it.

"Just start. Learn and apply what doesn't work."

-Patrick Schwarzenegger, Co-Founder of MOSH

Chapter 14

The Role of Community – How Founders Leverage Their Audience

The most successful brands aren't just businesses—they're movements. They don't just sell products; they create a sense of belonging, turning casual buyers into devoted advocates. When a brand fosters real community, its customers don't just purchase—they identify with it. They wear it, talk about it, and defend it like they would a favorite sports team. This is what separates brands that last from those that burn out after an initial wave of hype.

Community isn't built through ads or promotions. It's built through relationships, shared values, and a consistent connection between the brand and its audience. The strongest communities don't happen overnight. They're cultivated by founders who understand that customer loyalty isn't won through one-time transactions but through ongoing engagement, trust, and the feeling that customers are part of something bigger than just a product.

Some of the most iconic brands today started with nothing but a handful of dedicated early supporters. Stacy Madison, founder of Stacy's Pita Chips, built her brand by handing out free samples from her food cart in Boston, creating a direct connection with her customers before ever scaling into retail. She wasn't just selling pita chips—she was engaging with people, making them feel valued. That connection carried over as the brand grew, and by the time her chips hit store shelves, there was already a loyal community behind them. Stacy's early strategy of giving away free samples wasn't just about introducing people to the product—it was about creating an experience that customers felt personally connected to. People weren't just buying chips; they were supporting a brand they had interacted with firsthand.

Founders who understand the power of community prioritize authenticity. Customers can sense when a brand is trying to manufacture engagement versus when it's genuinely invested in its audience. Jaime Schmidt of Schmidt's Naturals built her brand from a kitchen experiment to a household name by leaning into her community. Selling her natural deodorant at farmers' markets wasn't just a way to move product—it was an opportunity to build relationships. She listened to feedback, talked directly to customers, and made every interaction feel personal. Even as she expanded into major retailers, she kept that grassroots feel, ensuring that customers never felt like just another number.

Successful brands don't just treat their audience as buyers—they treat them as collaborators. HexClad, for example, didn't just use digital platforms for selling cookware; they used them to educate, engage, and connect with their audience. Instead of treating their customers like passive buyers, they turned them into a passionate community of home chefs. Through behind-the-scenes content, cooking tutorials, and direct responses to customer inquiries, they made people feel like they were part of something. Customers weren't just buying a pan—they were buying into a lifestyle, a community of passionate home cooks who valued high-quality cookware. When brands go beyond simply selling and start adding value to their customers' lives, they build relationships that last.

Beyond digital engagement, real-world interactions create an even deeper connection. The strongest brands give customers ways to engage beyond a screen, whether through in-person events, pop-ups, or brand activations. These experiences allow brands to create tangible moments that customers remember long after they leave. This is something I've seen firsthand with the **Starting Small Summit**. Digital engagement is valuable, but nothing compares to in-person connections. Seeing a founder speak about their journey, shaking hands with like-minded entrepreneurs, and being part of a live discussion creates a level of engagement that no Instagram post or email campaign can replicate. The brands that win are the ones that understand the importance of blending digital and real-world interactions to build deeper, more meaningful relationships.

This strategy has also driven the success of DTC brands expanding into physical retail. Brands like Glossier and Allbirds have proven that brick-and-mortar retail isn't just about selling products; it's about creating a space where customers can connect with the brand in a way that's impossible online. These stores act as hubs where customers don't just shop—they engage. Exclusive product launches, workshops, and meet-and-greets turn retail spaces into community centers that reinforce brand loyalty.

At the core of any strong community is exclusivity. When customers feel like they're part of something special, their loyalty increases. The best brands cultivate this by offering early access, limited drops, and VIP experiences that make customers feel valued. Supreme built an entire brand around this idea—releasing limited quantities of each collection and creating a culture where owning a Supreme product felt like being part of an elite club. While not every brand needs to take this to the extreme, the principle remains the same: the more customers feel like they're part of something exclusive, the stronger their connection to the brand.

Loyalty programs take this further, turning one-time buyers into long-term supporters. However, the best programs don't just reward purchases; they build emotional connection. Sephora's **Beauty Insider** program, for example, isn't just about earning points—it's about access. Customers receive early product launches, invitations to exclusive events, and personalized recommendations that make them feel like insiders. The key isn't just in the rewards themselves but in how they reinforce the idea that being part of the brand's ecosystem is valuable beyond the product itself.

Brands that invite customers into their journey create an even deeper level of engagement. When people feel like they've contributed to a brand's growth, they become invested in its success. Crowdfunding platforms like Kickstarter and Indiegogo have shown how giving customers a stake in a product's launch can turn them into lifelong advocates. Beyond funding, brands that seek customer input—whether through beta testing, feedback groups, or interactive polls—strengthen their relationship with their audience. Customers who feel like they've helped shape a brand will go out of their way to support it.

Community isn't just external—it starts from within. Brands with strong cultures create stronger customer relationships. Companies where employees believe in the mission naturally pass that enthusiasm on to customers. A company like Sweetwater built its reputation not just on its products but on its legendary customer service. Founder Chuck Surack didn't just hire sales reps—he built a team of passionate musicians who could truly connect with their customers. That authenticity can't be faked. Customers can tell when a team genuinely loves what they're selling, and that energy is contagious.

At the core of every strong community is storytelling. People don't just connect with brands—they connect with stories. The brands that last are the ones that craft a compelling narrative and invite customers to be part of it. Patagonia, for instance, isn't just an outdoor apparel brand—it's a movement dedicated to environmental activism. Customers don't just buy Patagonia gear; they buy into a philosophy that aligns with their values. The result? Lifelong loyalty that goes beyond product features or price points.

The strongest brands aren't built on aggressive marketing tactics or endless discounting. They're built on relationships. They turn customers into communities, transactions into movements, and loyalty into advocacy. A brand with a real community doesn't have to chase every new marketing trend or rely on paid ads forever—its customers do the marketing for them. This kind of organic growth is what makes community-driven brands so resilient. They don't just compete on price or product features—they compete on emotional connection, and that's something that can't be easily copied.

Businesses that embrace this mindset don't just sell products; they build something bigger. They create brands that people don't just buy from but belong to. And in a world where customers have more choices than ever, that's what makes a brand irreplaceable.

"Be patient in what you want for yourself, but be impatient in how much you give to others."

-Jesse Cole, Founder of Savannah Bananas

Chapter 15

Why are Founders Storytelling? – Selling More Than a Product

Some brands sell products. The great ones sell stories. Storytelling isn't just a marketing tactic—it's the foundation of how customers connect with a business, understand its purpose, and ultimately choose where to spend their money. The brands that stand the test of time are those that don't just promote what they sell but communicate why they exist. A compelling story turns a product into something greater—it creates meaning, emotional investment, and loyalty beyond the transaction.

Every successful entrepreneur has a story, but not all know how to tell it. Those who do set themselves apart from the competition. When people feel emotionally invested in a brand's journey, they aren't just purchasing a product; they are aligning themselves with a vision. That's why storytelling is at the core of Starting Small—the founders I've interviewed didn't just build businesses, they built narratives that resonated with people on a personal level.

Joe Foster of Reebok didn't just create a sneaker company—he carried forward his family's legacy, navigating industry challenges and relentless competition to establish a brand that would be worn by athletes and everyday consumers alike. His journey was filled with struggles, including legal battles over trademarks, navigating an industry dominated by Nike and Adidas, and making key decisions that shaped the future of his company. When customers hear his story, they don't just see a sneaker brand; they see resilience, legacy, and an entrepreneur who refused to quit. That emotional connection is what makes people proud to wear Reebok, beyond just the performance of the shoes themselves.

Jaime Schmidt didn't set out to build a global natural deodorant empire. She was simply looking for a cleaner, more effective product for her family. As she started experimenting in her kitchen, she had no idea she was laying the foundation for a movement in personal care. When she started selling her products at farmers' markets, she wasn't just making sales—she was educating people on the importance of natural ingredients, listening to their concerns, and using their feedback to improve. That direct engagement built trust and made her brand feel personal. Even as Schmidt's Naturals expanded into major retailers, that sense of authenticity never faded. Customers didn't just buy deodorant—they bought into her belief that personal care products could be clean and effective without compromise.

In industries where competition is fierce, the right story can be the ultimate differentiator. A great product might attract attention, but a great story is what makes people stay. When customers understand a founder's journey—the sacrifices, the failures, the pivotal moments—they become invested in the success of the brand. They aren't just supporting a product; they are supporting a mission.

A brand's story is strongest when it is personal, transparent, and real. Too many companies manufacture origin stories that feel contrived, missing the mark on what actually builds trust. The best storytellers don't fabricate narratives—they embrace their unique journey, including the challenges, setbacks, and defining moments. Founders who communicate with vulnerability and honesty build brands that feel authentic and irreplaceable.

Chuck Surack of Sweetwater is a prime example. He didn't start with a massive business plan or investor backing. He started by recording demos in the back of his Volkswagen bus and treating every musician he worked with as if they were the most important customer in the world. His philosophy of "always do the right thing" became the backbone of Sweetwater's customer experience. Over time, that reputation turned into an undeniable competitive advantage. Sweetwater isn't just a retailer—it's a trusted partner for musicians, built on decades of doing right by its customers. That story is why so many loyal customers refuse to shop anywhere else.

But storytelling extends beyond the founder—it's woven into the DNA of the brand itself. Companies that understand this embed storytelling into every part of the business, from marketing campaigns to product descriptions to customer interactions. They don't just tell their own story; they help customers see themselves as part of it.

HexClad, for instance, doesn't just market itself as another cookware company. Instead, they frame their product as a solution to a long-standing kitchen frustration: the need for both nonstick convenience and stainless steel durability. By telling the story of how they innovated a new hybrid technology, they aren't just selling pans; they're selling a problem solved. That positioning makes their brand feel essential rather than just another option in a crowded market.

Great storytelling also builds anticipation. Some of the most successful brands create ongoing narratives that customers want to follow. Apple has mastered this. Every product launch isn't just about new features—it's about the evolution of their story, the next chapter in a journey that customers are already invested in. The anticipation, the attention to detail, the consistency—all of it reinforces the brand's identity and keeps people engaged.

Authenticity in storytelling doesn't mean oversharing—it means being intentional about how a brand communicates its values and mission. The best stories aren't just about what happened, but why it mattered. Founders who understand this use their story as a way to build trust and connection, rather than just as a tool for promotion.

Nike is another example of a company that has built its brand around powerful storytelling. Their campaigns don't focus solely on selling shoes; they highlight perseverance, grit, and the human spirit. The iconic "Just Do It" slogan isn't about a product—it's about a mindset. When customers buy Nike, they aren't just buying athletic wear; they're buying into the idea that they can push beyond their limits. The storytelling is aspirational, and that's why it works.

A well-told story also makes a brand memorable. Consumers are bombarded with marketing messages every day, and most of them are forgettable. But stories stick. The best brands create narratives that people remember, that they want to share, that make them feel something. That's why brands that master storytelling often grow through word-of-mouth—because their customers aren't just buying a product; they're repeating a story that resonates with them.

Customer stories can be just as powerful as founder stories. Brands that elevate their customers' experiences create a deeper level of engagement. A testimonial isn't just about how a product worked—it's about how it changed someone's life, solved a problem, or made them feel. Some of the strongest brands don't just tell their own stories; they amplify the stories of the people who use their products.

The best storytelling happens when a brand understands its audience on a deep level. It's not about pushing a narrative—it's about reflecting the values, aspirations, and challenges of the people it serves. Founders who get this right build more than businesses; they build communities of people who feel genuinely connected to what they're creating.

The brands that last aren't just selling—they are making people feel something. And when people feel something, they don't just buy. They believe.

"If in a good place, there's nothing better than building with family and friends."

-Jason Karp, Co-Founder of Hu (Hu Chocolate)

Chapter 16

Learning from Failure

Failure isn't a possibility in entrepreneurship—it's a certainty. Every founder, no matter how successful, has faced moments where everything seemed to be falling apart. The difference between those who make it and those who don't isn't avoiding failure—it's knowing how to respond to it. The best entrepreneurs don't just endure setbacks; they use them as stepping stones, learning more from what went wrong than from what went right.

One of the hardest things for any entrepreneur to accept is that failure is part of the process. No matter how much planning goes into a business, there will always be unexpected obstacles. Some are small—delayed shipments, an underperforming marketing campaign, or a bad hire. Others are massive—running out of cash, losing a key supplier, or a product launch completely flopping. What separates resilient founders is their ability to analyze failure, pivot when necessary, and keep pushing forward without losing sight of the long game.

Joe Foster of Reebok faced countless setbacks while trying to build his brand. Breaking into the athletic footwear industry wasn't just about making great shoes—it was about fighting legal battles over trademarks, convincing retailers to take a chance on a lesser-known brand, and competing against giants like Nike and Adidas. There were moments when it seemed like Reebok wouldn't survive, but instead of letting failures define him, Foster treated them as challenges to solve. His persistence ultimately turned Reebok into a global powerhouse. The lesson? Setbacks aren't the end of the road—they're part of the journey.

Stacy Madison of Stacy's Pita Chips also knows what it's like to hit a wall. Long before selling her company to PepsiCo, she was simply trying to keep up with demand. At one point, production issues nearly derailed her entire operation. Instead of panicking, she adapted—adjusting sourcing strategies, refining her manufacturing process, and staying laser-focused on quality. She knew that growth wasn't just about scaling fast—it was about scaling smart. Founders who survive tough moments aren't necessarily the most talented or the best-funded. They're the ones who refuse to quit.

Failure is often framed as something to avoid at all costs, but the reality is that setbacks are where the best lessons come from. The companies that last aren't the ones that never struggle—they're the ones that learn quickly and move forward without hesitation. The key is distinguishing between temporary challenges that can be fixed and structural problems that require a full pivot. Some failures teach you how to refine your business; others tell you it's time to change direction completely.

Jaime Schmidt built Schmidt's Naturals into a household name, but that success didn't come without early missteps. When she first started selling at farmers' markets, she had to constantly adjust her approach based on customer feedback. Some formulas didn't work, some branding decisions missed the mark, and some expansion efforts stretched the company too thin. But she stayed adaptable, taking every misstep as a lesson rather than a defeat. That mindset allowed her to refine her brand until it was strong enough to scale nationally.

The worst kind of failure is the slow kind—the kind where problems build up over time, and by the time you recognize them, it's too late. A business doesn't usually collapse overnight. It happens gradually—sales decline month after month, key employees leave, customer complaints increase. Many founders fail not because of a single catastrophic event, but because they ignore the warning signs and assume things will turn around on their own. A big part of surviving failure is catching problems early enough to do something about them.

Some founders fail because they scale too quickly. Growth can be just as dangerous as stagnation if it's not managed properly. Many businesses expand their team, their inventory, or their marketing budget before they have the revenue to sustain it. Suddenly, they're running out of cash, struggling to fulfill orders, or drowning in overhead costs. A product that had steady demand at a small scale might not hold up once it hits mass distribution. Some businesses don't fail because they weren't good ideas—they fail because they tried to grow before they were ready.

Others fail because they hold on too long to a bad idea. Entrepreneurs are naturally optimistic, which can be both a strength and a weakness. When you've invested time, money, and energy into an idea, it's painful to admit that it's not working. But one of the hardest lessons in business is learning when to let go. The best founders aren't just willing to push through challenges—they're also willing to step back and say, "This isn't working." That doesn't mean giving up on entrepreneurship; it means redirecting efforts into something with a stronger foundation.

There's a reason some of the most successful entrepreneurs failed before they found their big win. Many of the biggest companies today exist because the founders had already learned from previous failures. Evan Williams co-founded Blogger, sold it to Google, and then launched Odeo—a podcasting platform that flopped. But he took what he learned from Odeo and co-founded Twitter, which became one of the most influential platforms of its time. The ability to take failure in stride and apply its lessons is what separates long-term success from short-term attempts.

Failure also teaches resilience. The founders who succeed long-term aren't the ones who avoid failure—they're the ones who embrace it, learn from it, and use it as fuel. Every founder will have moments where they doubt themselves, where they feel like they're out of options, where quitting seems like the easiest path. The ones who push through those moments are the ones who eventually break through.

One of the most important ways to recover from failure is to avoid taking it personally. It's easy to see a business failure as a personal failure, but they're not the same thing. A failed product launch doesn't mean you're a bad entrepreneur. A business that doesn't work out doesn't mean you're not capable of building a successful one. The faster you can separate your personal identity from your setbacks, the faster you can recover and try again.

The smartest entrepreneurs treat failure like an experiment. They analyze what went wrong, extract the key lessons, and use that information to improve their next attempt. The worst thing an entrepreneur can do after a failure is nothing. Sitting in regret, overanalyzing the past, or being too afraid to try again only guarantees one thing—you stay stuck. The best move after a failure is forward.

It's also important to surround yourself with people who understand the entrepreneurial journey. Many people outside of the startup world don't get it. They see failure as final. They don't understand that setbacks are just part of the game. Having mentors, peers, or even employees who have experienced failure themselves can make a huge difference in how you recover. A strong network can remind you that failure isn't unique to you—it happens to every entrepreneur at every level.

Some failures are completely avoidable. There are certain mistakes that founders make repeatedly—ignoring financials, hiring too quickly, not validating their market, overcomplicating their product. Learning from others' mistakes can sometimes save you from making the same ones. But even the best-prepared founders will still encounter unexpected failures. That's why the ability to adapt is more valuable than the ability to plan.

The reality of failure is that it doesn't always feel like a learning experience in the moment. Sometimes it feels like a punch to the gut. Losing money, letting employees go, or seeing years of work unravel is never easy. But the ability to reframe failure—to see it as a necessary step rather than a dead end—is what allows the best founders to keep moving forward.

Setbacks aren't a sign to give up—they're proof that you're in the game. If you're failing, it means you're trying, experimenting, and taking risks. That's what entrepreneurship is. The only true failure is the failure to try again. The entrepreneurs who understand this don't just survive setbacks; they use them to build something even stronger.

"There's never going to be a perfect time to do anything. Find problems and fix them."

-Rob Schultz, Co-Founder of Ro(man)

Chapter 17

Exit Strategies – Selling, Acquiring, or Scaling Forever

Every entrepreneur eventually faces a crucial question: what's next? After years of building a company from the ground up, founders must decide whether to keep growing, sell, merge, or step away. There's no one-size-fits-all answer. The right decision depends on the business, the founder's goals, and the opportunities available. But one thing is certain—those who don't think about their exit strategy early on often find themselves unprepared when the time comes.

Some founders build their businesses with the clear intention of selling. They structure their company from day one with an acquisition in mind, keeping financials clean, creating scalable systems, and ensuring that the brand is attractive to potential buyers. Others grow organically, only considering an exit when the right offer lands in their inbox. And then there are those who never want to sell at all, preferring to build something that will last for decades under their leadership. Understanding these different paths—and the trade-offs that come with each—is critical for any entrepreneur.

Jaime Schmidt of Schmidt's Naturals built her company from a small kitchen experiment into a widely recognized brand sold in major retailers. When Unilever approached her with an acquisition offer, it wasn't just about the paycheck—it was about what was best for the brand and its mission. Selling to a massive corporation meant expanding Schmidt's reach and getting natural personal care products into the hands of more people. But it also meant letting go of control. That's a choice every founder considering an acquisition must weigh—are they willing to hand over their brand in exchange for growth?

Selling isn't always the right move, though. Many founders struggle after selling their companies, realizing too late that they weren't ready to step away. Some feel lost without the daily grind, while others regret how their brand changes under new ownership. Stacy Madison of Stacy's Pita Chips built an empire from a food cart, eventually selling to PepsiCo. While the acquisition was financially rewarding, it also meant no longer having control over the brand she built from scratch. Founders who sell must prepare for the emotional side of walking away, not just the financial outcome.

Not all exits involve selling to a large corporation. Some founders opt for a private sale, selling their company to an investor group, a competitor, or even their own employees. This route can allow for a smoother transition while maintaining the company's identity. Others choose mergers, combining forces with a like-minded brand to create something bigger. In some cases, acquisitions aren't planned but happen out of necessity. Companies that run out of cash, face industry shifts, or struggle with leadership changes often look for buyout opportunities as a way to salvage what they've built.

Then there are the founders who never want to sell. Chuck Surack of Sweetwater built his business not as a short-term venture, but as a lifelong passion. He didn't start Sweetwater to cash out—he built it to create something lasting. For founders like Chuck, the goal isn't to sell but to scale sustainably, ensuring the company continues to grow while maintaining its core values. The challenge for those who choose this path is succession planning. Without a clear strategy for leadership transition, even the strongest companies can falter when the founder steps back.

Scaling a company with no intention of selling comes with its own set of challenges. The business has to remain profitable, adaptive, and competitive while ensuring leadership transitions smoothly over time. A founder who wants their company to last decades must put systems in place to ensure that growth doesn't depend solely on their involvement. Many entrepreneurs fail to think about succession planning until it's too late, leading to companies that struggle or collapse when the founder exits. The most successful legacy businesses are those that build a leadership team capable of carrying the company forward without relying on a single individual.

Financial preparation is a crucial part of any exit strategy. Whether the goal is to sell or hold onto the company long-term, founders must keep their financials transparent, ensure profitability, and avoid unnecessary liabilities. A messy balance sheet, disorganized operations, or a business that's overly dependent on the founder makes an acquisition difficult and limits options for the future. Even if a founder isn't planning to sell, running a company as if it could be acquired at any moment forces financial discipline and operational efficiency.

Entrepreneurs who decide to sell must also be prepared for the process itself. A business sale isn't as simple as signing a contract and handing over the keys. It involves months—sometimes years—of negotiations, due diligence, and legal work. Potential buyers will scrutinize every part of the business, from financial records to customer retention rates. If a company isn't prepared, the deal can fall apart at any stage. The smartest founders prepare well in advance, keeping their financials clean, ensuring contracts are in place, and building a business that can run without their direct involvement.

For those considering a sale, valuation is one of the biggest factors. Many founders overestimate how much their company is worth, assuming that years of hard work automatically translate into a high price tag. But buyers don't pay for effort—they pay for financial performance, brand strength, and growth potential. Founders who want to maximize their valuation must prove that their business is scalable, profitable, and well-positioned for the future. A company with steady recurring revenue, strong customer retention, and a unique market position will always attract higher offers than one with inconsistent revenue and high operational risk.

Selling a business also comes with tax implications, legal considerations, and contractual obligations that many founders overlook. The structure of the sale—whether it's an asset sale, stock sale, or merger—has a huge impact on how much money the founder actually walks away with. Working with financial and legal advisors early in the process can prevent costly mistakes and ensure that the exit is structured in a way that benefits both the seller and the business.

Some founders who sell stay on as advisors or board members, while others walk away entirely. The level of involvement post-sale depends on the deal structure and the founder's personal goals. In some cases, buyers require the founder to stay on for a transition period to ensure a smooth handover. Other times, founders negotiate complete autonomy after the sale. Understanding the expectations post-sale is just as important as the terms of the deal itself.

Mergers present another route for founders who don't want to sell outright but see value in combining forces with another company. Merging with a competitor or complementary brand can create new growth opportunities, expand market reach, and improve operational efficiencies. But mergers also require careful alignment of company cultures, leadership styles, and long-term goals. A poorly executed merger can lead to internal conflict, customer attrition, and brand dilution.

Private equity and venture capital buyouts are another type of exit that some founders pursue. In these deals, investment firms acquire all or part of a company, often with the goal of scaling it quickly and selling it again at a higher valuation. While this can be a lucrative option, it also means giving up control. Many founders who take private equity deals find themselves pressured to hit aggressive growth targets, often at the expense of long-term brand equity. Understanding the trade-offs of working with financial investors versus strategic buyers is key in determining whether this type of exit is the right choice.

Regardless of the path chosen, the best exits are planned, not rushed. Founders who think ahead, structure their business for flexibility, and remain open to different opportunities put themselves in the strongest position when the time comes. Whether the goal is to sell, merge, or build a company that lasts for generations, having a clear strategy ensures that the decision is made on their terms—not out of necessity.

"Be in tune with your "head trash" - the negative emotions in your brain."

-Mike Salguero, Founder of ButcherBox

Chapter 18

Finding Balance – Entrepreneurship Without Losing Yourself

Entrepreneurship demands sacrifice. The long hours, the financial risks, the emotional rollercoaster—it's an all-consuming pursuit that can easily take over every aspect of life. Many founders pride themselves on their relentless hustle, wearing exhaustion as a badge of honor. But what happens when the business thrives, yet everything else falls apart? The truth is, success means little if it comes at the cost of personal well-being, relationships, and long-term happiness.

The idea that founders need to sacrifice everything to succeed is one of the biggest misconceptions in business. Yes, building something from scratch requires immense dedication, but burnout doesn't have to be the price of admission. The entrepreneurs who play the long game—the ones who don't just build successful companies but also fulfilling lives—are those who learn how to set boundaries, prioritize their health, and recognize that working smarter often beats working longer.

The problem is that many founders don't realize they're losing themselves until it's too late. They spend years operating at full capacity, assuming they can push through exhaustion, neglecting relationships, and ignoring the signs of burnout until they wake up one day feeling empty. The company might be thriving, but their personal life is in shambles. They don't know who they are outside of the business. Their identity is so wrapped up in what they built that stepping away, even for a moment, feels impossible. This is one of the biggest traps of entrepreneurship—not knowing where the business ends and the person begins.

Chuck Surack of Sweetwater built his company with an obsessive focus on customer service and quality. But even as Sweetwater grew into the largest music gear retailer in the U.S., he didn't let it consume him entirely. He understood that great leadership isn't about being available 24/7—it's about building a strong team, trusting others to take ownership, and ensuring that success isn't solely dependent on the founder. Delegation isn't just a business strategy; it's a survival tactic for entrepreneurs who want to sustain their passion without burning out.

The ability to delegate is one of the biggest differentiators between founders who scale successfully and those who collapse under the weight of their own business. Many entrepreneurs struggle with this because they're used to doing everything themselves. In the early days, they had no choice. They were the marketer, the salesperson, the product developer, the customer service rep. Letting go of that control is difficult. It requires trust—not just in employees, but in the systems and processes that keep the business running.

One of the most common struggles among founders is maintaining personal relationships. It's easy to justify missing family events, skipping vacations, or putting friendships on the back burner because "the business needs me." But over time, this approach backfires. Relationships aren't just a nice-to-have—they're essential to long-term success. Some of the most successful entrepreneurs I've interviewed on *Starting Small* have emphasized that their biggest regrets weren't business failures, but rather the moments they missed with the people who mattered most.

Many founders convince themselves that they'll prioritize relationships *after* they hit a certain milestone—after they reach a revenue goal, after they land a big partnership, after they exit the company. But that milestone keeps moving. By the time they finally feel "ready" to focus on their personal life, the damage is often done. The missed birthdays, the neglected friendships, the strained marriages—they can't be undone with financial success. Entrepreneurs who recognize this early make conscious decisions to build a business that supports their life, rather than one that consumes it.

Jaime Schmidt of Schmidt's Naturals experienced the intensity of rapid growth firsthand. As her brand expanded, the pressure mounted. The key to maintaining balance, she found, was learning when to step back, when to trust her team, and when to give herself permission to recharge. Founders who recognize that rest isn't a weakness—but rather a competitive advantage—are the ones who build companies that last.

Another key component of balance is knowing when to say no. Entrepreneurs often feel pressure to take every meeting, say yes to every opportunity, and push through every challenge no matter the cost. But spreading yourself too thin doesn't lead to growth—it leads to exhaustion. The best founders learn to protect their time ruthlessly, focusing only on what truly moves the needle.

It's not just about saying no to things that don't align with the business—it's also about saying no to tasks that don't require the founder's involvement. Every time an entrepreneur holds onto a responsibility they should have delegated, they limit their own ability to grow. The best founders understand that their role isn't to do *everything*—it's to focus on the highest-impact decisions while empowering their team to handle the rest.

Health is another area where entrepreneurs tend to cut corners, assuming they'll "catch up on sleep later" or "start exercising once things calm down." But stress, poor sleep, and neglecting physical health aren't just personal issues—they affect decision-making, creativity, and leadership. Some of the most effective business leaders prioritize fitness, meditation, or even just taking regular breaks as a way to stay sharp. Burnout doesn't just impact the founder; it impacts the entire company. A mentally and physically drained leader makes worse decisions, reacts poorly to setbacks, and creates a culture of stress rather than inspiration.

Beyond personal health, founders who don't take the time to recharge often lose the creative spark that made them successful in the first place. The ability to step away—to disconnect, travel, spend time with family, or explore interests outside of work—actually fuels better business decisions. Some of the most game-changing ideas don't come from working around the clock; they come in moments of stillness, when the mind has space to think freely.

Many founders resist stepping back because they fear losing momentum. They believe that if they're not constantly pushing, everything will fall apart. But businesses that are *only* dependent on the founder's nonstop involvement aren't scalable. They're fragile. A truly strong company is one that can operate smoothly even when the founder isn't in the trenches every single day.

There's a misconception that taking time off means slowing down, but in reality, it often leads to better execution. Many of the most influential entrepreneurs—whether in tech, retail, or media—attribute their biggest breakthroughs to stepping back and allowing themselves to think bigger. The problem is that many founders wait until they're already on the verge of burnout before realizing the importance of balance. By that point, the damage is often done—health suffers, relationships strain, and the business itself starts to feel like a burden rather than an achievement.

A founder's relationship with work also sets the tone for company culture. Employees take cues from leadership. If the founder is constantly working late, skipping breaks, and glorifying overwork, the rest of the team will feel pressured to do the same. But if the founder demonstrates that balance is a priority—by taking time to recharge, setting clear work-life boundaries, and showing that personal well-being matters—it creates a healthier, more sustainable workplace for everyone.

The founders who create lasting impact aren't the ones who sacrifice everything for short-term wins. They're the ones who pace themselves, recognizing that sustainable growth requires sustainable habits. Finding balance isn't about working less—it's about working with intention, knowing that success is a marathon, not a sprint. The best entrepreneurs don't just build businesses; they build lives that are worth living beyond the company they create.

At some point, every founder has to ask: What am I actually building this for? Success isn't just about revenue, market share, or industry recognition—it's about whether the life you're creating is one you actually want to live. The entrepreneurs who find fulfillment beyond the business are the ones who recognize that work is just one part of the equation. They make time for the people and experiences that matter, ensuring that success doesn't come at the expense of the things that make life meaningful.

Those who master this balance don't just build companies—they build legacies. They create businesses that thrive not because of constant sacrifice, but because they've designed them to work in a way that's sustainable. They learn to trust their teams, set boundaries, and prioritize their well-being—not just for their own sake, but for the long-term success of their company.

Because in the end, what's the point of building something great if you lose yourself in the process?

"Dream so big that people think you're absolutely crazy. When you tell someone what you're going to be doing, if they don't think it's a crazy idea, you're not thinking big enough."

-Naveen, Tech billionaire & Founder of Viome

Chapter 19

Long-Term Thinking – Playing the Infinite Game

Most businesses are built for the short term. Founders chase quick wins, rapid growth, and immediate profits, often without considering what happens five, ten, or even twenty years down the line. But the entrepreneurs who truly build something lasting—something that outlives them—think differently. They play the long game, making decisions that don't just serve their company today but ensure it remains relevant for decades to come.

Long-term thinking in entrepreneurship isn't about hitting arbitrary milestones or seeking a fast exit. It's about creating a company with staying power—one that evolves with time, adapts to industry changes, and prioritizes sustainability over short-lived success. This requires patience, vision, and the ability to avoid the distractions that come with short-term wins. The best founders don't just focus on scaling fast; they focus on scaling right.

Businesses that last aren't built on hype. They're built on strong fundamentals, disciplined execution, and a relentless focus on what actually matters. It's easy to get caught up in what's working right now—chasing whatever marketing trend is driving engagement, expanding into new product categories without a clear strategy, or spending aggressively on customer acquisition without considering long-term retention. But short-term tactics without a long-term foundation create fragile businesses. The companies that endure are the ones that play the game differently, resisting the temptation to prioritize speed over sustainability.

Chuck Surack, the founder of Sweetwater, didn't build his company with the intention of flipping it for a quick payday. He focused on serving musicians for life, ensuring that every customer interaction reinforced trust, quality, and an obsession with doing the right thing. That philosophy turned Sweetwater into a dominant force in the music industry, outlasting competitors that chased aggressive expansion without prioritizing customer loyalty. When businesses approach growth with an infinite mindset—one where they aren't just thinking about this year's revenue but about how to serve their customers for generations—their brand becomes something more than just a product. It becomes an institution.

The same philosophy applied to Joe Foster as he built Reebok. The company wasn't an overnight success. It took years of persistence, strategic partnerships, and brand-building before Reebok became a household name. Rather than chasing short-term wins, Foster played the long game—focusing on product credibility, athlete endorsements, and positioning his brand for longevity rather than fleeting success. Reebok didn't just ride trends; it shaped them, ensuring that the company would remain relevant even as competition grew fiercer.

The entrepreneurs who think in decades, not just years, understand that their reputation is one of their most valuable assets. It takes years to build credibility and seconds to lose it. Companies that last don't sacrifice their brand's integrity for short-term revenue spikes. They resist the pressure to cut corners, dilute quality, or compromise their values just to satisfy quarterly earnings targets. The strongest businesses understand that trust isn't something you can buy with marketing—it's something that has to be earned consistently over time.

This mindset extends beyond just external reputation—it influences how founders approach decision-making at every level. When leaders focus only on short-term metrics, they make decisions that may look good on paper but ultimately weaken their company. They might underpay employees to hit a profitability goal, invest in aggressive cost-cutting that hurts product quality, or push for rapid expansion without ensuring operational stability. These choices can boost revenue temporarily, but they often come at the expense of long-term brand equity.

Founders who prioritize longevity understand that growth isn't just about adding more customers—it's about keeping the ones they already have. Customer loyalty isn't built through aggressive acquisition strategies alone; it's built through consistency. The companies that dominate for decades are the ones that provide an unwavering level of quality and trust. They don't constantly pivot their messaging or reinvent their identity to chase trends. Instead, they reinforce what makes them different over and over again until it becomes deeply ingrained in the minds of their customers.

This is why the best businesses invest heavily in customer relationships. It's easy to treat customer service as an afterthought when sales are booming, but the companies that last are the ones that go above and beyond to create an exceptional experience at every touchpoint. Sweetwater's entire business model is proof of this. By prioritizing personalized service, technical support, and a level of care that far exceeds industry standards, they didn't just build a company—they built a brand that musicians trust for life. That level of commitment to the customer isn't just good business; it's the foundation of longevity.

Another defining characteristic of long-term thinkers is their approach to innovation. They don't just create one great product or service—they build a culture of continuous improvement. Jaime Schmidt didn't stop at one natural deodorant formula; she constantly iterated, expanded into new product lines, and ensured that Schmidt's Naturals stayed ahead of industry trends. Businesses that stand the test of time are those that never settle. They keep evolving, not out of desperation, but because they understand that relevance requires constant refinement.

Sustainable businesses also understand the importance of building strong teams. Many founders focus so much on growing their business that they neglect the people who make it possible. But companies that endure don't just have great products—they have great cultures. They create workplaces where employees feel a sense of purpose, where leadership fosters growth, and where people want to stay. Employee retention is one of the most overlooked aspects of long-term success. A revolving door of talent creates instability, knowledge loss, and cultural erosion. Founders who prioritize hiring the right people, developing their teams, and creating an environment where employees are motivated to stay build companies that are far more resilient.

Beyond internal culture, financial discipline plays a critical role in sustainability. Many companies fail not because their product isn't great, but because they expand too fast and lose control of cash flow. The best founders resist the pressure to overextend. They grow steadily, reinvest profits wisely, and ensure that their infrastructure can support each new level of expansion. They don't let investor pressure or market hype dictate their pace—they focus on building a business that will still be strong decades from now.

Businesses that endure also prepare for challenges before they arise. Economic downturns, industry shifts, and unforeseen obstacles are inevitable. But the companies that last are the ones that build resilience into their foundation. They don't rely on unsustainable growth tactics or assume that success will always come easily. They plan for the unexpected, ensuring that when the market shifts, they're in a position to adapt rather than react.

At its core, playing the long game is about resisting the distractions that come with short-term thinking. The greatest entrepreneurs don't build businesses for a single milestone, an IPO, or a buyout. They build something that can evolve, adapt, and continue thriving long after they've stepped away. True legacy isn't measured in revenue alone—it's measured in impact, reputation, and the ability to create something that stands the test of time.

Founders who embrace this mindset understand that building a lasting business requires patience. They're willing to forgo immediate gratification in favor of a stronger long-term position. They don't chase trends—they create them. They don't prioritize short-term wins at the expense of sustainability. They build for longevity, ensuring that what they create outlives them.

Ultimately, every entrepreneur must decide whether they are building something for the moment or something that will last. The ones who choose the latter may not see the fastest results, but they will see the most meaningful ones. Because the businesses that truly change industries, reshape culture, and leave a lasting impact aren't the ones that burned brightest for a few years—they're the ones that stood the test of time.

"Vulnerability and humility lead to a great mindset and the adaptability needed to be an entrepreneur."

-David Lester, Co-Founder of Olipop

Chapter 20

Lessons from 250+ Founders – Key Takeaways for Future Entrepreneurs

After interviewing over 250 of the world's leading founders, one thing has become clear: there is no single path to success. Every entrepreneur's journey is different—some stumble into an idea, while others meticulously plan for years. Some bootstrap with nothing, while others raise millions before they even launch. Some thrive on rapid growth, while others build slowly and deliberately. Despite these differences, common themes emerge—patterns that hold true across industries, experience levels, and backgrounds. The founders who succeed aren't always the ones with the best product or the perfect timing. They're the ones who make the right moves, adapt quickly, and refuse to quit when things go wrong.

The most important lesson? Just start. Nearly every founder I've interviewed has said some version of the same thing: if you wait for the perfect moment, it will never come. The most successful entrepreneurs weren't the ones with the best funding, the best connections, or the most experience. They were the ones who took action before they felt ready. They learned by doing, adjusted along the way, and embraced the discomfort of uncertainty. Perfectionism kills more dreams than failure ever will. It's easy to get stuck in the planning phase, waiting until every detail is figured out before taking the leap. But real progress happens when you put something into the world and start getting feedback. Most of the successful companies we know today didn't launch with their final version—they evolved through trial, error, and relentless iteration.

Resilience is everything. Every founder I've talked to has had moments when quitting seemed like the only option. Running out of money, dealing with manufacturing disasters, getting rejected by investors over and over—these aren't exceptions, they're the norm. The path to success is filled with setbacks that feel impossible in the moment. But the ones who make it through are the ones who refuse to let failure define them. They pivot when necessary, they push through self-doubt, and they keep going when most people would have given up. The difference between those who succeed and those who don't isn't talent, resources, or even luck. It's the ability to take a hit and keep moving forward.

No one builds alone. Despite the myth of the lone genius entrepreneur, every successful founder I've interviewed had people who lifted them up—mentors who offered guidance, co-founders who balanced their weaknesses, or early believers who gave them a shot. The best entrepreneurs surround themselves with those who challenge them, support them, and hold them accountable. They don't try to do everything on their own. They seek out people who are smarter than them in key areas and aren't afraid to delegate. Building a company isn't just about solving problems—it's about building the right team to solve them together.

Customer obsession separates good from great. Whether it was Chuck Surack at Sweetwater, Stacy Madison with her pita chips, or Jaime Schmidt at Schmidt's Naturals, the best founders didn't just sell products—they served people. They listened. They iterated based on real feedback. They went above and beyond to create experiences that customers wouldn't forget. When customers feel genuinely valued, they don't just buy a product—they become brand evangelists. And word-of-mouth is still the most powerful form of marketing. Building something people love isn't about flashy branding or viral marketing stunts—it's about delivering real value and proving, over time, that you care.

The best brands tell real stories. Every successful entrepreneur I've spoken to understood the power of narrative. People don't just buy products; they buy meaning, connection, and identity. Founders who openly share their struggles, values, and vision create something that goes beyond transactions—they create movements. Authenticity wins. Consumers today are more skeptical than ever, and they can tell when a brand is just chasing trends versus when it actually stands for something. The most enduring brands aren't just selling—they're inspiring. They give customers a reason to feel emotionally invested, and that connection creates lasting loyalty.

Playing the long game wins. The entrepreneurs who build lasting companies aren't chasing overnight success. They aren't obsessed with vanity metrics or short-term wins. They focus on sustainability, on treating people right, and on making decisions that serve their customers and teams for decades, not just quarters. The pressure to grow fast can lead founders to cut corners, compromise on quality, or burn through cash chasing quick wins. But the brands that truly last—the ones that outlive trends and competition—are the ones that play the infinite game. They don't just optimize for today; they make decisions with the future in mind.

Success comes from focus. The best founders don't spread themselves too thin chasing every opportunity that comes their way. They know what they do best, and they double down on it. Distraction is one of the biggest killers of momentum. I've seen founders dilute their brand by launching too many products too soon, entering markets they weren't ready for, or constantly pivoting without giving anything enough time to work. The ones who break through are those who stay laser-focused on their core strengths, perfecting one thing before expanding.

Execution matters more than ideas. People love to romanticize the idea of a "lightbulb moment," but the truth is, ideas are worthless without execution. Plenty of people have great ideas. The difference is that successful founders take action. They figure things out as they go, iterate quickly, and don't get paralyzed by uncertainty. The best entrepreneurs aren't afraid to get their hands dirty, sell their own product, and refine their process in real time. They don't waste years over-analyzing—because they know that real learning happens in the field, not in a business plan.

Culture is everything. One of the biggest mistakes founders make is thinking they'll focus on company culture "later," once they scale. But by then, it's often too late. Culture isn't about perks or office aesthetics—it's about the values that drive decisions when no one is watching. It's about how the team treats customers, how leadership handles adversity, and how employees feel about their work. The best companies prioritize culture from day one, knowing that a strong internal foundation leads to stronger external results.

Speed matters, but patience wins. The ability to move fast is an advantage, but sustainable growth requires patience. Some of the most successful brands took years before they became household names. Founders who expect immediate results often get frustrated and give up too soon. The ones who build for the long term understand that great businesses take time to develop. They resist the urge to force growth before they're ready. They don't chase shortcuts—they focus on getting things right.

Through all of these lessons, one thing remains true: starting small is never a disadvantage. The greatest businesses in the world started with an idea, a problem to solve, and a founder willing to take a risk. Growth comes from momentum, and momentum comes from simply beginning.

For those who dream of building something—whether it's a brand, a company, or a movement—there will never be a perfect time. There will never be a guaranteed outcome. But the path forward has been paved by those who have done it before, and if there's one thing they all agree on, it's this: the only way to get anywhere is to take the first step.

Acknowledgments

This book wouldn't exist without the hundreds of founders who have shared their stories with me through **Starting Small**, opening up about their struggles, breakthroughs, and defining moments. I am endlessly grateful for their honesty and willingness to share what most people never see.

To my family—thank you for your support, even when my schedule was packed with interviews and I had to miss some outings.

To the **Starting Small** community—you are the reason this journey has been possible. Every listener, every message, every conversation sparked from an episode has fueled my passion for storytelling and entrepreneurship.

And to Chuck Surack—your example of servant leadership and deep commitment to people has shaped the way I view business. Your story has been one of the greatest inspirations in my journey, and I'm honored to dedicate this book to you.

About The Author

Cameron Nagle launched Starting Small in January 2020 with the vision to share transparent startup stories to inspire and provide guidance for aspiring entrepreneurs that everyone starts small. Through a credible and fast growing list of recognizable brands, Starting Small has scaled to host the annual Starting Small Summit, flying in founders such as Reebok, Stacy's Pita Chips, Kodiak Cakes, and more. Starting Small has now covered the stories of 250 industry leading founders, amassing over $40 billion in annual revenue.

In 2022, Cameron relocated to LA to launch brain wellness startup, MOSH alongside co-founders Maria Shriver and Patrick Scwarzenegger, as the third member of the founding team. In their first year, MOSH generated +$6M in revenue, released 4 new flavor launches, and activated growth campaigns with Delta airlines, A-list celebrities and more. In 2023, Cameron also applied for Schwarzenegger and Shriver to go on

ABC's Shark Tank, in which you can see that appearance in Season 15.

Now, Cameron is back in Indiana. Relocating back to his roots was a long term decision for the growth of Starting Small and the summit locally and to make an impact on the entrepreneurship ecosystem in the Michiana community.